GREAT AMERICAN

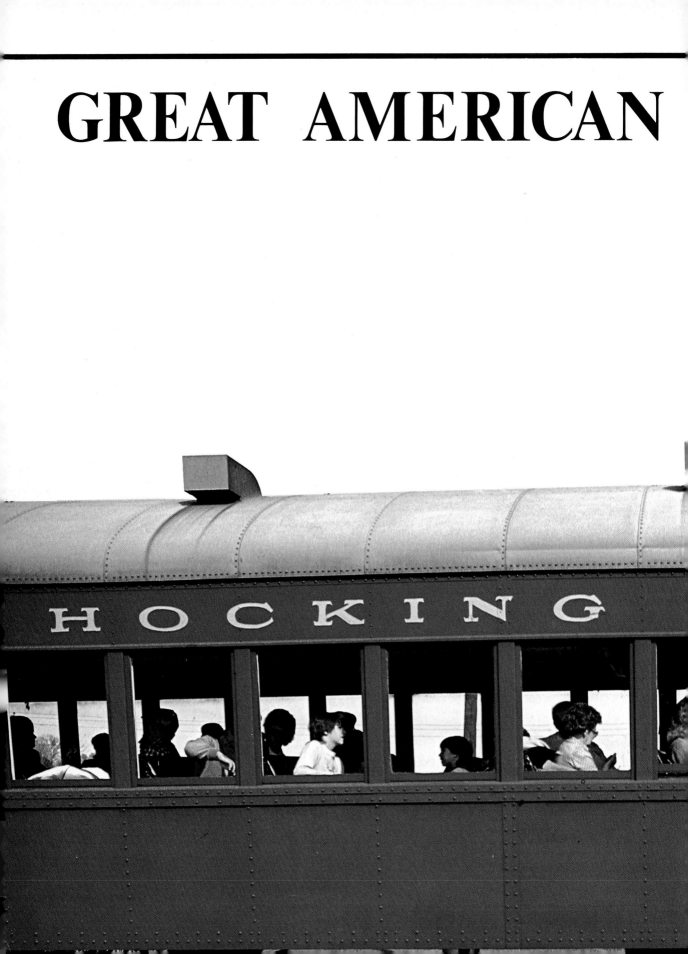

SCENIC RAILROADS

By TERRY BERGER and ROBERT REID
with a Foreword by Oliver Jensen

DESIGNED AND PRODUCED BY ROBERT REID AND TERRY BERGER

E. P. DUTTON • New York

Front cover: The Valley Railroad, Essex, Connecticut. Photograph Howard Pincus.
Page 1: The Valley Railroad, Essex, Connecticut. Photograph Howard Pincus.
Contents page: Conway Scenic Railroad. Photograph George W. Gardner.
Back cover: Strasburg Rail Road. Photograph George W. Gardner.

*All photographs not credited to a photographer are reproduced
courtesy of the railroad.*

Map: Lise Albertson / Tony Reid.
Editorial assistance: Stephen Brewer.

Published in the United States by E.P. Dutton, Inc.
2 Park Avenue, New York, N.Y. 10016

Library of Congress Catalog Card Number: 85-71299

ISBN: 0-525-48174-5

Published simultaneously in Canada by Fitzhenry & Whiteside Limited, Toronto

10 9 8 7 6 5 4 3 2 1

First Edition

A Robert Reid / Terry Berger Production

Typeset in Times Roman by Monotype Composition Company, Baltimore

Printed and bound by Mandarin Offset International, Ltd., Hong Kong

ALL ABOARD

*To Stephen D. Bogen and the Tourist Railroad Association
for their dedication to the preservation of railroads.*

FOREWORD

Oliver Jensen,
Chairman of
The Valley Railroad.
Photograph
John Lewis Stage.

This book belongs next to the Bible and the dictionary in the home of anyone who likes trains, who loves their dignity and power, whose back tingles when the melancholy whistle blows in the distance. Terry Berger and Robert Reid have done a great service for the history-minded, for they celebrate a group of magical enterprises that testify to the enduring grip the railroad has on the North American imagination. More than any other instrument, it opened the West, both in the United States and Canada.

Except along our littorals, it decided where our cities would go. It was our biggest business in the nineteenth century, and made almost all other business possible. It is in our blood. On the railroads shown in the pages to follow, it is possible to revisit the past. Getting there, on these restored lines, is not "half the fun." It is nearly all of it.

You can have almost any kind of railway experience on these lovingly tended lines. Some are very short, some hundreds of miles long like the Algoma Central of Ontario. The "Tweetsie" of Blowing Rock, North Carolina, would fit on a small farm. Blowing Rock! These little lines specialize in places with odd and romantic names—Montezuma, Orbisonia, Snoqualmie, French Lick, Cripple Creek. They run by steam, most of the time, although Puffing Billy comes in many shapes and sizes, from the tiny narrow-gauge locomotives on the Edaville Railroad in the cranberry-bog country at South Carver, Massachusetts (on two-foot-wide track) to the giant Royal Hudson of Vancouver, a continent away.

Some are former branch lines, redeemed from underbrush and rust by the strenuous efforts of volunteer track crews —like the Valley Railroad of Essex, Connecticut, which runs along the lower Connecticut River, or the Wolfeboro Railroad of New Hampshire, with its terminus at sprawling Lake Winnepesaukee. Some have stunning stations, like the Conway Scenic Railroad of New Hampshire, whose Victorian depot is all gold and white, dominated by two elegant towers.

On many of these tourist runs the visitor can enjoy scenery that is otherwise inaccessible, from the marshes, dunes and little villages where the Cape Cod & Hyannis chugs through the undeveloped parts of an otherwise crowded vacationland to the austere, dramatic canyon of the "Rio de las Animas Perditas" (River of the Lost Souls) where the narrowgauge steam trains of the Durango &

Silverton are still the only route. Its yellow wooden cars, although once almost abandoned, have been carrying the venturesome since the great Gold Rush days. For sheer drama it is hard to match the world's oldest cog railway, which has been running up Mt. Washington, the highest pinnacle in New England, since 1869; this sturdy antique is the model the Swiss copied for their breathtaking mountain lines. Pike's Peak has a cog railway too, reaching up—with the latest modern equipment—over 14,000 feet. In its conservative Yankee way, Mt. Washington is still in steam. On the Algoma Central one crosses unbelievably high trestles; on the Cass Scenic Railroad in West Virginia the game is to labor up the mountain on steep grades behind "Shay," or logging locomotives, odd-looking, powerful affairs with gears instead of the usual side rods. Getting there is indeed most of the fun, but it is also a matter of "how": relishing the wonderful prime movers, the gleaming, old-fashioned cars, the delights of antiquity in motion.

The model railroader, after he has gotten over the initial thrill of watching his little train simply circling about on a table, realizes something is lacking. He puts in a toy depot. And after a while he adds some trees, signals, and other miniature scenery. Perhaps a little village, a bridge, a water tower. So it is often with the creative and energetic enthusiasts who operate tourist railways. You restore your stations, you put in a village, you create a museum. You take advantage of what nature has provided, like the Roaring Camp & Big Trees Narrow-Gauge Railroad in California, with its majestic redwoods. Or like the Valley Railroad on the Connecticut River that put in a dock to meet riverboats, as railroads did generations ago when they came to water barriers, whether on rivers, lakes, or sounds.

One of the most interesting things to do when visiting the railroads in this book is to explore the yard and the repair shops; there is always someone around to tell you about the line's history. Indeed most of the enthusiasts you meet this way can trace the genealogy of any piece of equipment or rolling stock that catches your eye. The average passenger car you see is a veteran of many other railroads, often acquired one jump ahead of the scrap dealer. Yet the old-time car, unlike the tinny product of today, was built to last, and no matter how disheveled it may look on acquisition can be restored to look almost new. Engine and car shops at most tourist lines are full of masters of lost arts, which one must be if boilers are to be retubed, springs repaired, and car bodies made whole. They can do astonishing things with out-of-date tools, and with very little money. Nearly all the lines in this book have come back from the dead, or at least been saved from extinction, thanks to such skills and enthusiasms. "Angels" exist, and have financed some lines, but they are rare, and most of us in this business must earn our way at the ticket office.

The railroad buff, whether active in one of these enterprises or simply a passive visitor, has been on the American scene almost from the start. The Balti-

COMMON TYPES OF ENGINES USED ON THE SCENIC RAILROADS

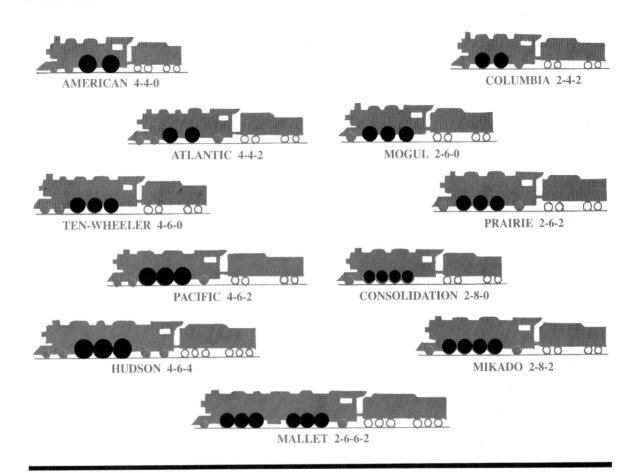

AMERICAN 4-4-0

COLUMBIA 2-4-2

ATLANTIC 4-4-2

MOGUL 2-6-0

TEN-WHEELER 4-6-0

PRAIRIE 2-6-2

PACIFIC 4-6-2

CONSOLIDATION 2-8-0

HUDSON 4-6-4

MIKADO 2-8-2

MALLET 2-6-6-2

more & Ohio ran photo excursions before the Civil War! The buff and his fellows packed many a "grand opening train" in the last century, watching the spike-driving and ribbon-cutting that marked those events. Nevertheless, railroad managements have never really understood the fan; even the public relations officers thought him a crank; he wanted to see, not the new diesel streamliner, shaped like a teardrop, but the old steam kettle that the company was about to discard. He wanted the company not to abandon the Broken Elbow branch and wrote his Congressman about it, besides showing up at public utility hearings to make trouble. Why couldn't he get a Ford like everyone else, management complained, and stop trying to make them keep the train running?

The fans still bother management, and they multiply every year. You can see them in great crowds at Strasburg, and South Carver, and Durango, and Conway. Who are they? Some of them, the younger ones, the children of the automobile age, have never ridden a train before, and yet they heed the call of the bell and the whistle, all of which proves that the railroad, with its glistening rails, and its great iron engine leaking steam at every pore, strikes a very deep chord in the nation's soul.

Oliver Jensen
Old Saybrook, Connecticut

CANADA

FRASER RIVER

BRITISH COLUMBIA

ROYAL HUDSON

B.C. RWY

LAKE WHATCOM RWY

PUGET SOUND AND SNOQUALMIE RR

WA

COLUMBIA RIVER

OR

MT

ND

ID

SD

MISSOURI RIVER

WY

M

THE SKUNK RR

NV

NE

SIERRA RWY

YOSEMITE MT. SUGAR PINE RR

UT

CO

MANITOU AND PIKE'S PEAK COG RWY

ROARING CAMP & BIG TREES RR

COLORADO RIVER

CRIPPLE CREEK & VICTOR RR

KS

DURANGO & SILVERTON RR

CA

CUMBRES & TOLTEC RR

PACIFIC OCEAN

AZ

NM

OK

TX

HAWAII

LAHAINA-KAANAPALI & PACIFIC RR

MAUI

TEXAS STATE

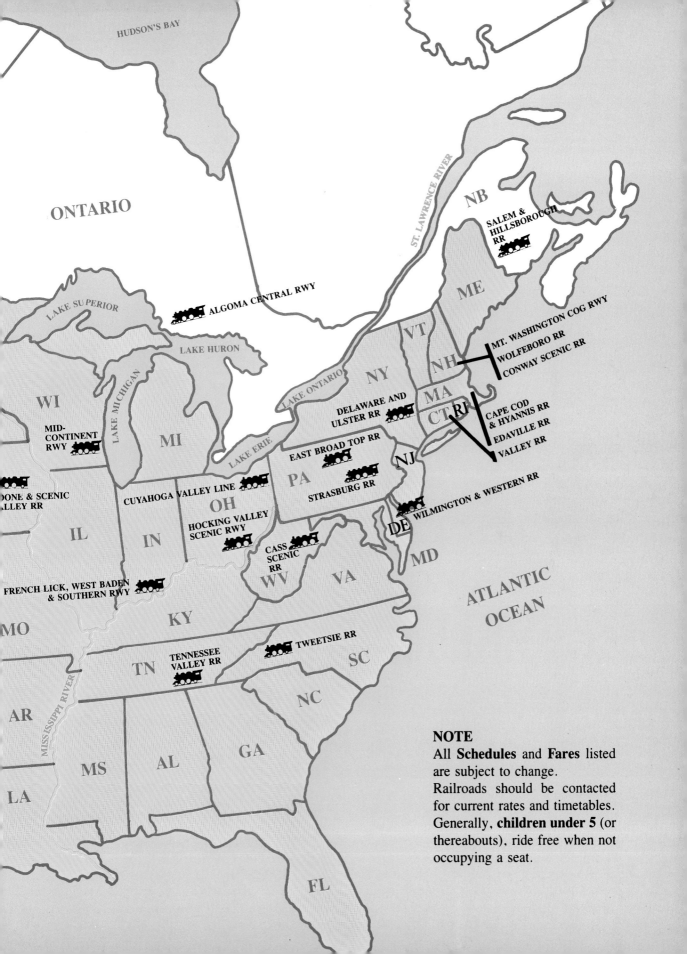

HUDSON'S BAY

ONTARIO

LAKE SUPERIOR

LAKE HURON

ST. LAWRENCE RIVER

NB

SALEM & HILLSBOROUGH RR

ME

VT

ALGOMA CENTRAL RWY

LAKE MICHIGAN

MT. WASHINGTON COG RWY
WOLFEBORO RR
CONWAY SCENIC RR

NH

WI

MID-CONTINENT RWY

MI

LAKE ONTARIO

NY

MA

CT RI

CAPE COD & HYANNIS RR
EDAVILLE RR
VALLEY RR

DELAWARE AND ULSTER RR

BOONE & SCENIC VALLEY RR

CUYAHOGA VALLEY LINE

LAKE ERIE

EAST BROAD TOP RR

PA

NJ

OH

IL

IN

HOCKING VALLEY SCENIC RWY

STRASBURG RR

DE WILMINGTON & WESTERN RR

CASS SCENIC RR

MD

FRENCH LICK, WEST BADEN & SOUTHERN RWY

WV

VA

ATLANTIC OCEAN

MO

KY

MISSISSIPPI RIVER

TENNESSEE VALLEY RR

TWEETSIE RR

SC

AR

TN

NC

MS

AL

GA

NOTE
All **Schedules** and **Fares** listed are subject to change.
Railroads should be contacted for current rates and timetables.
Generally, **children under 5** (or thereabouts), ride free when not occupying a seat.

LA

FL

Mt. Washington Cog Railway

For 120 years, the summer stillness at the foot of New Hampshire's Mount Washington has been interrupted by the distinctive toot of the whistles on half a dozen coal-fired, steam-driven engines that push passenger coaches up a track to the top of New England's highest mountain.

The oldest steam powered cog railway in the world—and now the only one—the railway was invented and promoted as a tourist attraction by Sylvester Marsh, who opened it on July 4, 1869. It has been going strong ever since.

Marsh's idea, which he successfully demonstrated in 1858 with a scale model, and again in 1866, when the first engine actually pushed a flatcar loaded with potential investors up a short length of track, is remarkably simple. The cog engines use a wheel with teeth that engage a cog rail in the center of the track and literally pull the engine up the mountain, where the average grade is 25 per-

"The second greatest show on earth"

cent and the maximum grade is 37½ percent. For more than a century, the little engines were tried, tested, refined, and perfected, and except for the orientation of the boiler, very little has changed in their basic design—a design that is unlike anything else that runs on rails.

The trip itself, along three miles of track, takes three hours to complete. All upbound trains make a stop for water, and they pull off on a siding to allow descending trains to pass.

At the peak, there are television transmitting towers, a weather observatory, and the recently built Sherman Adams building, with a cafeteria and an observation tower. Trains stop long enough for passengers to purchase refreshments and to take in the view that P. T. Barnum called "the second greatest show on earth!" On a clear day, when you can see all six New England states, Canada, and almost New York City, you know that Barnum wasn't kidding!

The descent takes about forty minutes under the guidance of a highly skilled brakeman controlling the passenger coach. The record, three minutes on a sled, is not recommended.

At the base station, passengers waiting for a train, or those who don't want to take the trip to the top, can visit the Cog Railway Museum and marvel over the collection of tools and equipment used in building the railway and view the scale models and a slide show.

Mt. Washington Cog Railway, Route 302, Bretton Woods, Mount Washington, New Hampshire 03589; (603) 846-5404. A 3-hour ride, operating for 120 years, with breathtaking views of New England. **Schedule:** daily from mid-May to mid-Oct.; hourly trains until 3 hrs before sunset; extra trains during peak times. Reservations encouraged. **Fares:** round trip to summit, incl. admission fee, $24*; one-way descent from summit, $10; admission only, $2, includes shuttle train, museum, gift shop, cafeteria. **Location:** from I-93 take Route 302 to Bretton Woods, where a large sign directs you 6 miles east to base of Mount Washington. **Of special note:** weather can be extremely changeable, sometimes obscuring the view. Schedules are subject to these conditions.

bove, Jacob's Ladder, 4600 feet above sea level, is a trestle 3½ miles long with the steepest grade on a ilroad—37½ per cent. ight, the base station, showing an early engine with the boiler laced vertically. Photographs Ron Johnson.

Conway Scenic Railroad

The most photogenic country depot

Left, everything at the Conway Railroad is beautifully restored. This view from the roundhouse shows a Prairie 2-6-2 engine on the turntable, some fine old passenger coaches, and the wonderful depot in the background. Above, hot-air balloons cast off on the North Conway Common in front of the depot. Photographs Ron Johnson.

Conway Scenic Railroad runs over a restored portion of the Conway Branch, which at one time linked the Conways with Boston's North Station. The Portsmouth, Great Falls and Conway Railroad, a subsidiary of the Eastern Railroad, constructed the line in 1872–73. When, a century later, the Boston & Maine Railroad terminated regular service and deeded the depot and entire terminal area to a realtor, the lot was bought up by two North Conway businessmen who vowed to save it from commercial exploitation.

Dwight Smith, a railfan from Portland, Maine, discovered the depot on a Boston & Maine "snow train" outing. It was love at first sight. Meeting with owners Reed and Levy, he formulated his plans for operating a railroad museum. It took almost seven years of determination and, ultimately, legal intercession before the Boston and Maine agreed to sell the upper end of the Conway branch. But when they did, volunteers arrived from all walks of life to make Smith's train ride a reality.

Highlights of the ride include panoramic views across the intervale to White Horse and Cathedral Ledges, as well as to Moat Range. On a clear day there is a magnificent vista of Mount Washington, the north-east's highest mountain peak. Passing dairy farms, one of which has 500 head of Holstein, the train goes over a small trestle that allows cows to pass under the tracks, then descends a 3.2-percent grade, the steepest main-line grade in New Hampshire. The train crosses over several bridges and over Moat Brook on a wooden trestle, from which Pine Hill and Redstone Lodge loom into view.

Built in 1874 and restored a century later, the North Conway station is one of the most picturesque country railroad stations in the country.

In addition to the depot, the grounds include a roundhouse with four stalls, a turntable, and an old freight house that currently houses a large H-O gauge model railroad layout.

Rolling stock, when not in use, is kept on various sidings. Equipment includes an 0-6-0 locomotive, built originally for the Grand Trunk Railway in 1921, and a 1920 Baldwin 2-6-2. The twelve passenger cars include a 1904 Delaware & Hudson baggage-coach combination, two early 1900 Laconia open-air coaches, and a wooden Pullman car circa 1898.

Conway Scenic Railroad, P.O. Box 947, North Conway, New Hampshire 03860; (603) 356-5251. A 1-hour, 11-mile trip into the golden age of railroading over a line built 113 years ago. **Schedule:** weekends May to early June; daily mid-June to late Oct.; trains depart depot rain or shine at 11 A.M., 1, 2:30, 4 P.M. **Fares:** $4.50, children half. **Location:** North Conway is on Route 16/US-302. **Of special note:** the Roundhouse with locomotives and turntable, and the elegant Pullman observation car.

Wolfeboro Rail Road

The pride and joy of the Wolfeboro is its steam locomotive

There are three important dates in the story of the Wolfeboro Rail Road in New Hampshire.

The first is 1872, when the brand new railroad was opened to traffic along its 12.03 miles. The first train consisted of five coaches and a gleaming 4-4-0- American-type locomotive supplied by the Eastern Railroad, which ran the line for the town. That first train, packed full of riders, was a forerunner of the eight passenger trains a day that eventually ran up and down the line, met by carriages from local inns and taverns. With baggage, mail, newspapers, and freight, Wolfeborough was a hive of activity beyond the wildest dreams of the town fathers, who had first conceived of and promoted the railroad as a spur to business. For a while, because the Wolfeborough connected to the Eastern Railroad and thence to the Boston and Maine, fast but economical rail transportation made it possible to work in Boston or Portland while living in Wolfeborough and commuting daily.

The second important date is somewhere around 1917, when the "ugh" was dropped from both the town and railroad name. Wolfeborough became Wolfeboro.

The third date is 1972—exactly 100 years after that maiden trip—when the Wolfeboro began operating as a tourist railroad, once again carrying passengers and freight as it had until 1936, when passenger service had ceased.

The pride and joy of the new Wolfeboro Rail Road is its steam locomotive—a 2-6-2 Prairie built in 1926 by the Baldwin Locomotive Works in Pennsylvania for the Tatum Lumber Company in Mississippi. The name lettered on the tender,

however, was the Bonhomie & Hattiesburg Southern, to which it was leased for most of its life. The locomotive is of such a vintage that it suited perfectly a Japanese-made television series on the 1905 Russo-Japanese war that was filmed at Wolfeboro.

Of direct interest to tourists, though, are the line's scheduled train trips and its various specials, one of which is the Sunset Diner, offering a variety of cuisine, from lobster clambakes to chicken barbecues. Sometimes there is live music and dancing.

Wolfeboro Rail Road, R.F.D. No. 2, Wolfeboro, New Hampshire 03894; (603) 569-4884. A 2-hour steam train trip through New Hampshire countryside. **Schedule:** weekends May 19 to June 10; daily June 16 to Oct. 21; special dinner and fall foliage trips. **Fares:** information from railroad, incl. specials. **Location:** on Route 28 in southeastern New Hampshire. **Of special note:** train connects at Wolfeboro with the boat "Mt. Washington" for a 3-hour cruise on Lake Winnepesaukee.

Left, the Prairie steam locomotive plowing snow in a crisply cold winter scene and, below, backing into the engine house beside Wentworth Lake. Photographs Ron Johnson.

Salem & Hillsborough Railroad

Named after the Prince Consort at the height of the Victorian era, the Albert Railway ran 45 miles from Salisbury, New Brunswick, down the Peticodiac River, through Hillsborough to Albert. The big customer on the line was the Hillsborough plant of the Canadian Gypsum Company, which shipped barrels of gypsum, and later wallboard, until it closed down in 1979. The railroad, then owned by the Canadian National Railway after a long history of bankruptcies and name changes, was abandoned in 1982. The New Brunswick Division of the Canadian Railroad Historical Association jumped in, and a new railroad was born with the purchase of 9½ miles of track from Hillsborough to Pine Glen Road.

With a million-dollar government grant, the purchase and lease of equipment started in earnest, and by November,

Turning back the hands of time

Hillsborough, New Brunswick

1983, three steam engines, a diesel, and fifteen other pieces of stock rolled into the tiny town of Hillsborough. The official opening of the new railroad, named the Salem & Hillsborough, took place in June, 1984, exactly 100 years after the first opening, and 20,000 riders thrilled to their first ride that year on the vintage equipment. Sixteen more pieces were added later in the year, in addition to a water tower and turntable at Salem.

The dynamic energy driving the railroad started with a group of railfans in Saint John, New Brunswick, where Abel Bastarche first dreamed of running a steam engine in the province, and in 1980 started collecting train·equipment with a group of friends. They came up with a crane, baggage car, boom car, and caboose. In 1981 they combined their interest with a group in Moncton, another New Brunswick town, and two more baggage cars were added to the list.

All of this early equipment, added to the flood of engines and rolling stock that came later from the federal funding, has produced a substantial steam railroad. Running along the upper end of the Bay of Fundy, site of the world's highest tides, the scenic line includes a curved wooden trestle, as well as views of woods, fields, and wild fowl seen as the train steams across the gentle maritime countryside.

Salem & Hillsborough Railroad, P.O. Box 70, Hillsborough, New Brunswick, Canada E0A 1X0; (506) 734-3195. A project of the Canadian Railroad Historical Association, N.B. Division, with 9½ miles of old Salisbury and Harvery Railroad track snaking along the Petitcodiac River. **Schedule:** daily in July and Aug. with 3 trips a day from 1:30 to 4:30 P.M.; weekends only in Sept. and Oct. **Location:** Hillsborough is in southeastern New Brunswick on Route 114 south of Moncton. **Of special note:** the Dinner Train and the October Fall Foliage runs, each a 2½ hour ride.

Left, No. 42 steaming over the trestle at Dawson Road, midpoint on the line. Photograph Rick Hodgson. ***Below,*** *through Hillsborough hay fields, the 1899 engine pulls a 1930s Canadian National coach and an ex-boxcar-turned-coach. Photograph Ray Knapper.*

The Cape Cod & Hyannis Railroad

Below, train crossing to Buzzards Bay on the Cape Cod canal railroad bridge, which lifts between the towers to let boats pass. Right, Mark Snider, the railroad's owner, perched on the back platform of a 1920s parlor car. Photograph Richard Howard. Bottom, train en route from Hyannis to Buzzards Bay.

A ride that cannot be duplicated

Bypassing traffic jams, the Cape Cod & Hyannis Railroad provides nostalgic train service to Hyannis, Sandwich, Buzzards Bay, Falmouth, Cataumet, and Monument Beach. On a route that cannot be duplicated by car, the train meanders through untouched countryside past farmlands, cranberry bogs, salt marshes, the dunes of Sandy Beach, and Sandwich Village (Cape Cod's oldest town), past ocean vistas, and over the famous vertical-lift railroad bridge that spans the Cape Cod Canal. Covering a total of forty-five miles, the ride captures the beauty of Cape Cod's legendary scenery.

The coaches date back as far as 1912 and include the elegant "Nobska" and "Presidential" parlor cars. The "Nobska," built in 1912 and which Mark Snider, the railroad's twenty-eight-year-old owner, refers to as a "Victorian masterpiece," is elegantly appointed with mahogany dining tables, recliners, carpeting, leaded glass, and crystal chandeliers. Used during the Winter Olympics at Lake Placid, this car is the diner on the railroad's popular dinner excursions.

THE CAPE COD & HYANNIS RAILROAD

The 1926 "Presidential" observation car has oversize arm chairs, carpeting, private bar, air-conditioning, and a unique observation platform that is similar to the one President Truman used on his famous whistle-stop campaign. Other equipment includes seven coaches dating to 1924 including a combine that has been converted into a standing bar car and a tavern car purchased from the Canadian National Railway.

The railroad provides eighteen optional round trips, including connections to Martha's Vineyard, to the Heritage Plantation, to shopping, and to canal cruises. Meals are available for groups. In fact, many passengers just ride to relax with a cocktail or well-prepared dinner while savoring the sights and luxuriating in the pleasures of the new golden age of railroading.

The Cape Cod & Hyannis Railroad, 1252 Main St., Hyannis, Massachusetts 02601; (617) 771-1145. Summer passenger service between Hyannis, West Barnstable, Sandwich, Buzzards Bay, Cataumet, Falmouth, and Greater Boston offers a scenic and painless alternative in getting to Cape Cod for some of the 12 million yearly visitors. **Schedule:** Daily service to all points mid-May through October; write for detailed schedules and fares. **Location:** depots at Hyannis, Buzzards Bay and Falmouth and connections with ferries at Buzzards Bay and Martha's Vineyard. **Of special note:** 1912 Nobska parlor car, ornate Victorian with plush arm chairs and leaded glass.

Above, Train passing through Pocasset on way to Falmouth. *Left*, en route from Buzzards Bay to Falmouth. *Right*, nothing could be finer than dinner in the diner. Photograph Walt Kiley.

Edaville Railroad

A fairyland of 200,000 Christmas lights

When steam powered railroads were being abandoned in the 1930s and 1940s, Ellis D. Atwood saw an efficient way to service his cranberry plantation. Rescuing equipment from the scrapper's torch, he bought up track and rolling stock and readied it for service in his cranberry bogs.

World War II delayed Atwood's plans but he started his railroad soon afterward. The tracks were just two feet apart and fit well along the tops of the dikes that separated the cranberry bogs. Boxcars and flatbeds helped Atwood harvest and maintain the 1,800-acre plantation.

Word of the railroad spread, and steam enthusiasts requested rides. Atwood, a dyed-in-the-wool rail buff, accommodated them. As ridership mounted, Atwood realized that he had a popular tourist attraction. Using his three initials, he formed the Edaville Railroad. At the time of Atwood's death in 1950, the railway had evolved from a working freight line to a busy passenger line. Begun as a memorial to him, the railroad's Christmas Festival transforms this bit of New England into a fairyland with 200,000 blinking colored lights.

Sold to F. Nelson Blount, a man who shared Atwood's love of the railroad, the Edaville prospered. Blount later went on to establish "Steamtown USA" in Vermont. Because he had originally planned to locate Steamtown in Edaville, he moved B & M locomotive 1455, the streamliner Flying Yankee, and many smaller engines there.

After the tragic death of the forty-nine-year-old Blount in a plane crash in 1970 the line was sold to present-owner George Bartholomew. Bartholomew, who had worked summers at Edaville, loved trains and had a background in public relations. He expanded the site into a family-fun park. Now, in addition to the five-and-a-half miles of narrow-gauge railroad, there is the Heritage Museum, with a collection of railroad memorabilia, antique fire engines, and vintage Americana; a re-created nineteenth-century village; a steam display; a miniature model T turnpike; an 1859 carousel that once ran on steam; and a petting zoo.

But the train is the main attraction. As it circles around a little cove at one end of a reservoir, it passes a whistle post, where, as has every train since 1950, it blows its whistle twice in memory of Edaville's founder.

Edaville Railroad, South Carver, Massachusetts 02366; (617) 866-4526. There are many things of interest to children—miniature cars to drive, animals to pet, trolleys and carousels to ride—but the 5½ mile narrow-gauge train ride is still the centerpiece of a serious railroad. **Schedule:** May, weekends and holidays, noon to 5 P.M.; daily June through Labor Day, 10 A.M. to 5:30 P.M.; after Labor Day, daily during Fall Foliage Season and Cranberry Harvest to Oct. 31, but diesel engines only on weekdays; Christmas season daily from Nov. 7 to Jan. 4, except Thanksgiving and Christmas day. **Fares:** general admission incl. train $6, children half. **Location:** on route 58 off I-495 south of Middleboro or 1 exit north of junction with I-195. **Of special note:** Railfans weekend and railroad flea market; Antique and classic auto show; Custom car show; Christmas festival.

Above, A triple header through the bogs pulled by two Baldwins and a 1913 Vulcan. Photograph Ron Johnson. Right, passengers get to see workers in the cranberry bogs in action. Far right, working engines hissing steam in the winter are a wonderful sight.

The Valley Railroad

The look and feel of a railroad in its heyday

The Connecticut River is not only very long, which is in fact what "Connecticut" means in the Algonkian Indian tongue, but in its lower reaches, past Hartford's towers and Middletown's old-fashioned Yankee waterfront, it grows exceedingly beautiful. Because there is no city at its mouth, it flows unspoiled through green hills and pleasant villages until it pours into broad Long Island Sound. Dotted with sails and shipping, the river has reminded many travelers over the years of the Hudson or the Rhine, but without the building and industry that have disfigured these busier waterways.

This setting alone would distinguish the Connecticut Valley Railroad from other tourist lines. Built along the great river's west bank, it opened in July 29, 1871, was swallowed up like most little companies into the busy New York, New Haven and Hartford Railroad, lost money for decades in this thinly settled land, carried its last passengers in 1933, and finally expired in the 1960s. The rusted tracks and rotting ties were grown over with weeds and saplings when an energetic group of volunteers, determined to re-create the look and feel of an American branch-line railroad in its heyday, raised a little money and went to work in the old rail yard at the pretty seafaring town of Essex. On July 29, 1971, exactly a century after the Connecticut Valley Railroad opened, while bands played and orators extolled the achievement, an authentic steam train once again whistled her way north out of the restored Essex depot. To be sure, she only went four miles and pulled just three restored cars, but this was the start.

Left, a stop at Deep River, on the run from Essex to Chester, lets passengers take a riverboat ride on the Connecticut River. Photograph Howard Pincus.
Right, *the plush parlor car Wallingford for first-class passengers. Photograph Ed Bohon.*

Today, the Valley Railroad, southern New England's only steam railroad, has grown into Connecticut's third-largest attraction for travelers, just a bit behind Mystic's historic seaport and its aquarium. Its trains can now meet Amtrak's at the northeast corridor stop at Old Saybrook, and the volunteers are still pushing northward, heading for Haddam and Middletown and dreaming, eventually, of restoring the original railroad in its entirety. There are five authentic old steam engines now, and the trains run seven or eight cars on frequent schedules through spring, summer, the fall-foliage season, and on December weekends before Christmas for the festival of lights, when Santa Claus moves through the cars greeting throngs of young people.

Everything is as it once was, and in the view of an occasionally grumpy old-timer, a little better. The seventy-year-old cars are handsomely restored; the engine gleams with gold striping, shiny black paint, and polished brass. There is a grand parlor car with leaded glass, swivel seats, and a bar, and occasionally, for special parties, a private car with a brass-enclosed observation platform. There is a restored 1910-era freight train, a museum, a gift shop and much more to fascinate a railroad buff in the yard and shops.

But the prize that sets the Valley Rail-road apart even further is that, as in days of long ago, every train meets a riverboat at its dock in Deep River for a cruise to parts of the river that are to be appreciated no other way. From Gillette's castle, home of the eccentric actor who popularized the role of Sherlock Holmes, to the shady reaches of mysterious Selden's Creek, or to East Haddam, dominated by the towering Victorian building of Goodspeed's Opera House, a fine bouquet of Americana can be savored as visitors return, again by train, to the starting point at Essex. It is a trip through history, by land and water, that can be experienced nowhere else.

Valley Railroad Company, Railroad Avenue, Essex, Connecticut 06426; (203) 767-0103. A 10-mile trip along the Connecticut River from the old seaport town of Essex to East Haddam, the home of the Goodspeed Opera House. Rail trip is about 1 hour, and the river cruise another hour. **Schedule:** 4 to 6 trains per day on weekends from first Sat. in May to June 15, then daily to Labor Day and daily except Mon. and Fri. through last Sun. in Oct. Runs weekends Thanksgiving through Christmas. **Fares:** $5 train and $8 train/boat; children less, parlor car extra; group rates, seniors rates, charter rates. **Location:** from east or west on Connecticut Turnpike (I-95) take exit 69 to Route 9 north and take exit 3 and follow signs to "Essex Steam Train." From Boston, New York, New Haven, Amtrak stops at Old Saybrook. **Of special note:** the latest locomotive, the "Samuel Freeman," a big Pacific from the Florida East Coast Railroad.

Delaware and Ulster Rail Ride

A rich and glamorous history

When the Penn Central Railroad sold the rails for scrap and the buyer tore up fifteen miles of track, few people expected ever to see a train running again on the Catskill Scenic Trail. But a grant from a public-service foundation turned that around. It awarded $3 million to buy the right-of-way back and revive the old Ulster and Delaware line.

The line had a rich and glamorous history. It started the booming Catskill resort industry when the scenic trail opened in 1871. The visitors who came to the famous, grand-scale resort hotels with Saratoga trunks, valises, grips, and hat boxes were prepared to spend the summer. At the peak of its operations, in 1913, the old *Ulster and Delaware* carried close to 700,000 passengers. But the last passenger train ran on the line in 1954, freight service was halted in 1976, and the venerable old railroad was abandoned.

Nicknamed the Red Heifer, because of its dark red color and side-to-side motion, the new line's engine is a combination diesel, freight, and passenger car. It once carried children to school, milk to creameries, and passengers and

Above, the Arkville depot will delight any rail fan. **Left,** trains must be the most photographed of human inventions, and the Red Heifer is no exception. *Photographs Don Bishop.*

livestock to various points—often all at the same time! A J. J. Brill 1928 model, it still has its wood-burning stove for heat, and its original smoking and non-smoking passenger seats.

The attractive depot at Arkville houses railroad displays, a gift shop, and a multimedia slide show. A permanent exhibit offers a brief history of the Ulster and Delaware Railroad and highlights the various attractions of the Catskill Scenic Trail.

The Catskill Scenic Trail is a roughly defined area that falls primarily in Delaware County. It includes a variety of scenic and historic attractions and activities: places to camp, hike, fish, ski, and golf, as well as such historical sites as the Jay Gould Church with its Tiffany windows, and the Hudson River Maritime Museum.

Delaware & Ulster Rail Ride, P.O. Box 243, Stamford, New York 12167; office (607) 652-2821, depot (914) 586-DURR. Trips from Arkville to Fleischmanns and Highmount revive the scenic train trip people took at the turn of the century. **Schedule:** May 25 to June 24, Thur. through Mon.; daily June 27 to Sept. 2; Sept. 5 to Oct. 20, Thur. through Mon.; 2 to 4 trips per day morning and afternoon—check for times. **Fares:** Fleischmanns $4; Highmount $6; children half. **Location:** on Route 28 near Margaretville, go 45 miles west at exit 19 of New York State Thruway. **Of special note:** the Arkville depot.

Right, engineer Vic Stephens and conductors Alan Gavette and Mike Thomas.

Strasburg Rail Road

Where all the stockholders are vice-presidents

Train time at the century-old Strasburg station. The locomotive at left is the famous Pennsylvania Railroad record holder from early in this century. Photograph Howard Pincus.

The Strasburg Rail Road carries passengers through the heartland of Lancaster County's beautiful Pennsylvania Dutch countryside. A ride on the coal-burning steam train blends in perfectly with the lifestyle of the Amish, who cultivate the lush farm land much as they did at the turn of the century. Living as simply as possible, they try to be self-sufficient, shunning such modern conveniences as electricity and automobiles. Gentle folk, they observe a way of life that has disappeared elsewhere.

The Strasburg Rail Road, a venerable institution, was founded in 1832 during Andrew Jackson's first term as President. The railroad continued to grow with the nation, it's existence dictated by changing times. At the turn of the century, most of its passenger traffic was diverted to a trolley line built between Lancaster and Strasburg, and regular passenger trains were discontinued. But freight kept the road solvent.

During the 1950s, improved highway transportation put the Strasburg into the red. By 1957, in addition to dwindling revenues, a series of storms and hurricanes wrecked the line; furthermore, it had become part of the Homsher estate, whose heirs viewed putting money into the train as throwing good money after bad.

STRASBURG RAIL ROAD

During those dark years, Henry K. Long, an industrialist and railfan from nearby Lancaster, was endeavoring to save the historic railroad. He tried to organize a group to purchase the property and restore and operate the railroad, but potential investors rebuffed him when it was disclosed that shares would sell for $450 a piece. Miraculously, someone got the idea of making every stockholder a vice-president. The gimmick worked, and in 1958, Long, acting as trustee for the purchasing group, tendered a check to the Homsher estate for $18,000. The railroad was born again.

When the present stockholders rescued the railroad in 1958, its power resources consisted of one twenty-ton gasoline-mechanical locomotive, whose wheels were so worn that the ICC would not permit it to run. Today the Strasburg possesses what is perhaps the best-maintained stable of steam power in the United States. In addition to the four steam locomotives it owns, it maintains and operates two more through long-term lease arrangements with the Railroad Museum of Pennsylvania. These two locomotives are classics—an American 4-4-0 numbered 1223 built in 1905, and an Atlantic 7002, formerly the 8063, a 4-4-2 sister to the original 7002 that in 1905 set the world's speed record for a reciprocating steam locomotive (127½ miles an hour on the head end of the Pennsylvania Special across open stretches of Ohio).

On the nine-mile round trip to Paradise, passengers ride in comfortable coaches equipped with coal-oil lamps and pot-bellied stoves. One, an elegant observation car, was featured in the film "Hello Dolly," starring Barbra Streisand.

As the train whistles for Carpenter's Crossing, there seems to be an echo after each blast. The conductor tells passengers that they are hearing the whistle of a ghost train on the other side of the hill—just four miles southwest of the crossing, a little narrow-gauge railroad once ran from Quarryville to Oxford.

Below, No. 1223 heads up a grade out of Groff's Grove. Photograph Ron Johnson.

Right, engineer Irvin White at the throttle of No. 90. Below, the Pennsylvania Railroad No. 7002 Atlantic climbing a grade at Carpenter's, Pennsylvania. Photographs Howard Pincus.

Strasburg Rail Road, P.O. Box 96, Strasburg, Pennsylvania 17579-0096; (717) 687-7522. Ride America's oldest short-line railroad through the scenic Pennsylvania Dutch Amish country. **Schedule:** (rain or shine) weekends 3rd Sat. in March through last Sun. in April, incl. Good Friday and Easter Monday; daily 1st week in May through last full week of Oct.; weekends Nov. and 1st 2 weekends in Dec. (featuring Santa Claus). There are at least 4 trains per day every hour from 12 to 3 P.M. and additional trains in high season and on holidays, the earliest at 10 A.M. and the latest at 7 P.M. Check full schedule. Trip takes 45 minutes. **Fares:** $4, children half. **Location:** south to Lancaster on US-222 from Reading Interchange of Penn. Turnpike; east from Lancaster on Route 30 to Route 896; south to Strasburg and east on Route 741 to depot. **Of special note:** the state-run Railroad Museum of Pennsylvania, and the Red Caboose Motel nearby, the only place in the world you can sleep in cabooses.

East Broad Top Railroad

At the end of World War II, and even before the East Broad Top narrow-gauge line was abandoned, railfans became increasingly aware of the uniqueness of the East Broad Top Railroad in central Pennsylvania. It became common practice for them to descend via car or Pennsy passenger train, marvel at the squat six-wheelers, ride the weekday mixed train, and poke around the intriguing relics of nineteenth-century railroading. An obliging crew would often hold up a train until a photo was shot. The faithful even showed up on Saturdays and during the annual two-week miners' vacation to ride the M-1, which replaced the steam trains. Starting in 1946, railfan extras were operated on Sundays.

Built in 1873, the East Broad Top Railroad was designed to move coal from the Broad Top mines. The fine grade of semi-bituminous coal was hauled to Mt. Union, where it was transferred from narrow-gauge cars and shipped over the Pennsylvania Railroad. The line survived until 1956 as a coal hauler, long after similar railroads had been abandoned. Last orders were issued on April 6, 1956.

Within a few months, the East Broad

Intriguing relics of nineteenth-century railroading

Top Railroad was sold to the Kovalchick Salvage Company. But the anticipated cannibalization of the line failed to materialize. For years nothing happened, except that grass, brush, and trees started to grow and flourish over the full length of the railroad.

In 1959, in nearby Orbisonia, the bicentennial committee started looking for a drawing card for their forthcoming

Left, View of the yards from the coal tower, looking towards the main building complex housing the roundhouse and station. Below, No. 15 taking on water. Right, the depot, much as it was over six decades ago. Photographs Thomas G. Klein.

EAST BROAD TOP RAILROAD

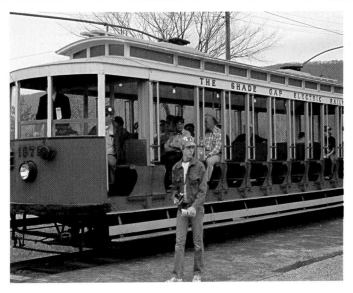

celebration. The members quickly realized that not every town had a genuine narrow-gauge railroad. Nick Kovalchick and Roy Wilburn, his operating vice president, were quick to cooperate. With former employees of the railroad and volunteers they miraculously reversed the effects of the railroad's inactivity. Quick to respond, fans and tourists appeared from all directions. And when the bicentennial was over, the trains continued to run on weekends well into the fall.

Later, rails were relaid on the roadbed of the old Shad Gap Branch, stretching out of Rockhill, so visitors can take

Above, the restored trolley line, which operates on weekends and holidays. Right, EBT is especially proud of passenger coach No. 8, from the Boston, Revere, Beach & Lynn Railroad. Below, an assemblage of equipment steaming back and forth for the photography buffs. Photographs Thomas G. Klein.

brightly colored standard-gauge trolley cars to the steam train depot.

The East Broad Top is a complete railroad system, from telegraph to turntable to eighty-ton locomotives. Its equipment and operations are typical of traditional railroading in the days of steam. And its continued existence is a tangible reminder of an unhurried age of men of steel, iron steam locomotives, and wooden passenger coaches. Long after the demand for coal has waned, the East Broad Top has developed a newer and quite different market—enthusiastic tourists and railfans. The romance and excitement of narrow-gauge steam lives on.

East Broad Top Railroad, Rockhill Furnace, Pennsylvania 17249; (814) 447-3011. A 10-mile, 50-minute trip through picturesque Aughwick Valley coal country. **Schedule:** trains run on the hour, 11 A.M. to 4 P.M. on weekends in June, daily July and August, weekends Sept. and Oct. **Fares:** approx. $5; children half; group rates. **Location:** from west or east on Pa. Turnpike take exit 13 north on Route 522 to Orbisonia. From east or west on I-80 take exit 24 or 23 south to join Route 22 to Mount Union, and then 11 miles south on Route 522 to Orbisonia. **Of special note:** steam locomotives open to inspection in the original 8-stall roundhouse.

Wilmington & Western Steam Railroad

Autumn Leaf Excursions, Ghost Trains, Santa Claus Specials

Another special run is the time for Christmas lights—at the station, atop the engine (old 98, an American type), and on many homes along the route. Photographs Thomas G. Klein.

Both the name and route of the Wilmington and Western Railroad are identical with its historical predecessor. Chartered in 1869 to provide public transportation for rural families between Wilmington and Landenberg, Pennsylvania, the original railroad, which ran a distance of twenty miles, was subsequently incorporated into the Baltimore and Ohio system.

By all economic standards, this road should not have been built. Earnings from its initial operations were $50,045.41, compared to the $816,821.11 cost of construction and equipment. Unforeseen costs of excavation—such as the Wooddale cut, which was blasted through 900 feet of solid rock in 1871—did much to bankrupt the infant railroad.

Since 1966, the Historic Red Clay Valley, Inc., a nonprofit corporation, has been operating steam passenger service along the line under the original Wilmington and Western name. Dedicated to promoting interest in the Red Clay Valley's ecology, cultural, and economic history, the primary objective of the corporation has always been the railroad.

Present-day and bygone images spring into mind along the Wilmington and Western's route: Red Clay Creek, Fells Spice Mills, Woods Ironworks, Brandywine Springs (formerly a favorite resort for fashionable summer tourists), two grist mills, Hercules, Garrett's Snuff Mills, and Jackson's Quarries.

Surprisingly, the railroad has the second-largest privately owned motive power roster east of the Mississippi. It has eleven steam locomotives, one electric locomotive, and four locomotives with internal-combustion engines. Among the railroad's locomotives is a pre-World War I Alco 4-4-0.

Donald Callendar, the Historic Red Clay Valley's dynamic executive director, has expanded train rides to include Great American Train Robberies, Bar-B-Que Chicken Specials, Autumn Leaf Excursions, Mother's and Father's Day Specials, Ghost Trains, and Santa Claus Specials. Delaware's largest flea market is held on the Greenbank station's grounds on weekends, weather permitting. The Greenbank station also provides passengers with a snack bar and gift shop.

Volunteers lovingly run, maintain, and restore the railroad's equipment. Track Superintendent Skip Small calls his track maintenance crew the "Historic Red Clay Valley Health Club." Small provides invigorating field exercises in tie-pulling, ballast shoveling, and spike-pounding three times a week at no charge.

Wilmington & Western Steam Railroad, P.O. Box 1374, Wilmington, Delaware 19899; (302) 998-1930. Operating railroad of Historic Red Clay Valley Inc. demonstrates a genuine steam railroad similar to the original one that served New Castle County in the latter half of the 19th century. **Schedule:** every Sunday, May through October, at 12:30, 2, and 3:30 P.M. Great American Train Robbery 1 Sun. a month; Autumn Leaf Specials last 3 Sat. in Oct.; Halloween Ghost Train the Sun. before Halloween; Santa Claus Special Fri., Sat., Sun., last weekend in Nov. by reservation only. **Fares:** $3, children $2; mothers, fathers, and veterans free on their holidays. **Location:** Greenbank Station on outskirts of Wilmington near the junction of Routes 2 and 41. **Of special note:** there is an illustrated catalog of the impressive roster of steam engines and an annual calendar of interest to railfans.

The discovery of iron ore in the mountains of North Carolina, coupled with the great railroad boom that had started at the end of the Civil War, brought Tweetsie to the Blue Ridge Mountains. By the end of 1916, the road went from Johnson City, Tennessee, to a terminus in Boone, North Carolina, sixty-six miles in all. For half a century, the narrow-gauge engines and miniature cars tweeted past homes, mining communities, and farms as conductors rattled off romantic names such as Sycamore Shoals, Pardee Point, Cranberry, Minneapolis, Montezuma. You didn't have to walk to a station if you wanted to get on; you merely flagged down the train.

After the Cranberry Coal and Iron Company closed in 1929, the railroad's only tasks were carrying mail, transporting logs, and hauling passengers. The Tweetsie managed to survive despite the death of the mines, the stripping of forests, and the growing competition of trucking. But the rains did her in. In August 1940, torrential rains battered the mountain country of North Carolina; there was no escaping the path of the onrushing water. It washed out the railroad's tracks and ended the Tweetsie's day.

Some of her cars were converted into gaudy diners on southern highways; others were shunted off to quiet sidings where they gathered dust.

Gene Autry once had an option on this train

Tweetsie Railroad

In 1950, when the Tweetsie officially passed from the scene, nostalgia enthusiasts were beginning to talk about the "old days." Clubs of railroad buffs were springing up to immortalize and salvage the memory of the railroads of the past—particularly the narrow-gauges.

Three men in Virginia were among them: a surgeon, a former railroader, and a feed-and-coal dealer. Seeking out used narrow-gauge equipment, they met with success, solely from the East Tennessee and Western North Carolina. After purchasing the only locomotive, coach, and observation car left, they had them transported to Harrisonburg, Virginia. Two years later, when Hurricane Hazel washed away much of the roadbed, the venture ended in failure.

Hollywood actor Gene Autry took an option on the train and talked about moving it to California. But in 1955,

Crossing the old wooden trestle is a highlight of the three-mile trip.

The train is the main attraction in a turn-of-the-century outing.

Grover C. Robbins, Jr., a North Carolina businessman from Blowing Rock and Lenoir, bought Autry's option and purchased Tweetsie. For its triumphant return to the hills of North Carolina, Governor Luther F. Hodges proclaimed a "Tweetsie Homecoming Day."

Today the Tweetsie Railroad is the keystone of a theme park that encompasses a wealth of family activities. The three-mile train ride in open-air coaches is pulled by a coal-fired steam locomotive. Passengers witness reenactments of a train holdup, an Indian raid, and other live action from early railroad days.

In addition to the train ride there is a chair lift to the "Tweetsie Mining Company," gold panning, and a petting farm. The park re-creates a turn-of-the-century outing with rides, arcades, general store, bank, fire house, blacksmith, and its train depot, an exact replica of one of Tweetsie's original stations.

Tweetsie Railroad, P.O. Box 388, Blowing Rock, North Carolina 28605; (704) 264-9061. A 3-mile rail trip behind finely preserved coal-fired steam engines, with all the action of the early railroad days re-enacted amid historic settings. **Schedule:** full operation with all shows on weekends from Memorial Day to end of Oct. and weekdays 2nd Monday in June through mid-August. Partial operation (train and some other activities) during weekdays rest of time to end of Oct. **Fares:** a general admission ticket of $8 covers train ride and some other activities; children slightly less. **Location:** between Boone and Blowing Rock, exit west at mile post 291 off US-221/321. **Of special note:** live entertainment at Tweetsie Palace.

Tennessee Valley Railroad

In 1959, a small group of Chattanooga, Tennessee, railfans who were concerned with the disappearance of the steam locomotive and the passenger train from the railroads of America organized the Tennessee Valley Railroad Museum. For eight years they devoted themselves to collecting whatever equipment was obtainable by donation and to seeking a permanent site for the construction of an operating railroad in the Chattanooga area. The search ended successfully, in 1969, when the Southern Railway System gave the museum a four-acre tract in East Chattanooga. The land was adjacent to the original Southern main line, which was opened in 1856, but had long since fallen into disuse.

Tennessee Valley Railroad volunteers began the arduous reconstruction of the railroad. What might have taken a commercial railroad about four months to complete took volunteers nearly twenty

Photography R. M. Soule.

Volunteers worked nearly 20 years to complete it

years. Today, however, the Tennessee Valley Railroad Museum stands as the only full-size operating railroad museum in the state, and it provides Tennessee's only regularly scheduled passenger service by steam locomotive.

The six-mile, forty-five-minute round trip operates near the original East Tennessee, Virginia & Georgia Railroad right-of-way. Crossing the Chickamauga Creek, the train goes over the Tunnel Boulevard Bridge and on through 986-foot Missionary Ridge Tunnel, which is one of the oldest railroad tunnels in Tennessee and the only "horseshoe" tunnel in the state. Confederate and Union soldiers fought for this vital connection to Chattanooga during the Civil War. The trip ends at the East Chattanooga depot.

The 1910-era depot at East Chattanooga is a faithful re-creation of a typical small-town station. Complete with passenger shed, waiting room with pot bellied stove, ticket office, and gift shop, it includes many parts from the recently demolished Athens, Tennessee, depot. It is air-conditioned and has indoor plumbing—a slight departure from total authenticity. The depot was completed in 1980.

The railroad operates six main-line excursions yearly. One of the most popular has been the Dogwood Arts Festival Special, a two-day excursion from Chattanooga to Knoxville and return. Green-and-gold steam engine 4501, a 1911 Baldwin Mikado pulls the train through the Tennessee countryside, which passengers can glimpse from an open observation car or the train's own dining car.

"Travelers' Fare," cooked-on-the-car breakfast, lunch, and dinner, is served in the diner, supplemented by tasty snacks and sandwiches from a commissary car.

The Chattanooga Choo-Choo, a Hilton Hotel complex, incorporates the magnificent former Southern Railway terminal in Chattanooga. It has been reopened as a stunning twenty-four-acre complex of shops, restaurants, gardens, an elaborate model railroad site, and travelers' accommodations, including twenty-four vintage Pullman sleeping cars that have been transformed into forty-eight Victorian suites.

Tennessee Valley Railroad, 4119 Cromwell Road, Chattanooga, Tennessee 37421; (615) 894-8028. A 6-mile train ride between 2 stations, with a very active museum at the East Chattanooga terminus with a variety of railroad equipment and memorabilia. **Schedule:** weekends March 30 to June 10; daily June 10 through Labor Day, then weekends until Dec. 1. Museum hours 11 A.M. to 4:30 P.M. and 1 to 4:30 P.M. Sundays with 4 to 6 trips between those times. **Fares:** $4.95, children $2.95. **Location:** Chattanooga Depot, 2200 North Chamberlain Ave., 10 minutes drive from downtown. **Of special note:** the green and gold Southern 2-8-2 Mikado 4501, whose restoration is such an interesting story a book has been written about it.

No. 4501, ex-Southern Railroad, getting up steam for an early morning excursion.

The immaculate ex-Southern 2-8-0 steaming off the East Chattanooga turntable.

Cass Scenic Railroad

A treasure-trove of priceless Shays

Left, the Cass's lightly laid, winding track is the Shay's natural habitat. Right, views of a busy railroad photographed by Thomas G. Klein, including the rustic lookout, below, at the mountain-top terminus.

Once central to the logging history of West Virginia, the Cass Scenic Railroad is a living museum, a window on the past. Visitors experience the raw power of steam as they climb through rugged wilderness, listen to stories that bring the logging era to life, and visit the fascinating steam locomotive shops to see priceless Shays being maintained.

Built as a logging railroad to haul red spruce and hardwood, the roadbed has incredible grades that reach 11 percent, even with switchbacks. Such grades, combined with sharp curves and roughly laid, uneven track, require a special type of locomotive. The Shay, gear-driven rather than rod-driven like the ususal locomotive, was specially designed to handle the job by Ephraim Shay, a Michigan inventor, who was a logger himself.

Riding on trucks (assemblies of wheels) very much like those on a freight car, the Shay can run on almost any kind of track. In addition, each wheel of the Shay is powered by a drive shaft so the entire weight of the locomotive supplies adhesive power to the rails. The Shay, slow but powerful, served the Cass lumber industry valiantly for sixty years.

In 1960, when railroad logging was no longer viable, the mill shut down and the railroad was to be scrapped. Dismantling of the line began, but fortunately the historic railroad was saved from extinction through the efforts of local businessmen, state legislators, and the West Virginia Department of Natural Resources, which purchased the whole railroad for $142,500. For this the state received twelve miles of track, three locomotives, ten flatcars, a water tank, four camp cars, three motor cars, and other railroad miscellany.

It wasn't until 1963 that Cass began hauling tourists. At first, many locals

Above, Shay No. 4, is a very impressive, powerful locomotive, also shown, at left, in the yards. Photographs Howard Pincus. Right, Shay No. 6, just about the largest ever built, on loan from the Baltimore & Ohio museum in Baltimore. Photograph Thomas G. Klein.

CASS SCENIC RAILROAD

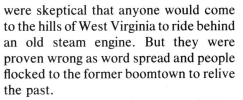

were skeptical that anyone would come to the hills of West Virginia to ride behind an old steam engine. But they were proven wrong as word spread and people flocked to the former boomtown to relive the past.

The Shay locomotives are priceless antiques that have been kept running much longer than the manufacturer intended. The oldest is Shay number 5, which came to Cass new in 1905. The newest is number 6, built in 1945 and used on the train to Durbin. It was the last one of its type ever built by the Lima Locomotive Works in Lima, Ohio. Weighing 162 tons, it is one of the largest Shays ever constructed. The total locomotive roster includes nine steam engines, two diesel units, and two more

Shays that were recently purchased from a defunct railroad in North Carolina.

The town of Cass was purchased in 1978, and people can now actually spend their vacations in a West Virginia company town.

Cass Scenic Railroad, P.O. Box 75, Cass, West Virginia 24927; (304) 456-4300. Three different trips ranging from 1½ to 4½ hours through scenic mountain country on a preserved logging railroad operating a rare collection of powerful old Shay engines. **Schedule:** daily except Mondays from May 26 through Labor Day and weekends in Sept. and Oct. Trains various times of day beginning 11 A.M. **Fares:** $6 to $9, children less; group rates. **Location:** in eastern West Virginia, off Route 28/92 from exit south of Green Bank or north of Dunmore. **Of special note:** the town of Cass, owned by the railroad and restored to accommodate tourists overnight.

Hocking Valley Scenic Railway

A *non-profit, all-volunteer railroad*

Dedicated to preserving historic railroading, the Hocking Valley Scenic Railway is a nonprofit, all-volunteer organization. Since its founding in 1972, members have repaired the track, maintained the locomotives and cars, and run the train on part of the original main line of the Hocking Valley Railway.

The Lake Superior and Ishpeming Railroad formerly used the line's 1916 Baldwin steam locomotive for hauling trains to Great Lakes' ore ships in upper Michigan. Known as a "Consolidation," because of its 2-8-0 wheel arrangement, the engine is one of the heaviest and most powerful of its type ever constructed.

Coaches used by the Hocking Valley Scenic were run originally on the Erie and Rock Island Railroads. The rolling stock also includes an open-air car and a gondola converted with special seats and safety railings. A restored wooden caboose from the Chesapeake and Ohio is on display.

The railway's station is typical of the many depots that the original Hocking Valley Railway built. A unique project, its construction was made possible by funds from the Baird-Stuart Foundation. A member of the community donated logs, which students at the milling operation of Hocking Technical College processed into lumber. The depot houses a museum, souvenir shop, and ticket office, and is decorated during the Christmas season for the annual holiday train rides with Santa, when Christmas music, stories, poems, and treats for the children complete the visit.

Conkle's Hollow, a deep, rocky gorge less than thirty minutes from the railroad, is well worth a visit. The mile-long trail through the gorge is picturesque and extremely rugged. Hikers ford a small stream several times as the path winds its way over and around large sandstone rocks.

Old Man's Cave, on Ohio route 664, is rich in local folklore and natural beauty. Years ago a creek in the park gouged its way through the Black Hand sandstone and created a gorge. The park was named for Richard Rowe, a hermit who moved into the cave shortly after the Civil War and remained there until his death.

*Above, the new depot is typical of the original ones built by the Hocking Valley Railway. The large Consolidation locomotive, **left**, taking on water, **right**, weighs over 220 tons when fully loaded with 13 tons of coal and 10,000 gallons of water.*

Hocking Valley Scenic Railway, P.O. Box 427, Nelsonville, Ohio 45764; weekdays (513) 335-0382, weekends (614) 753-9531. Two trips, one of 25 miles and another of 10 miles, provide the nostalgic sound of steam locomotive whistles echoing in the scenic hills of southeastern Ohio. **Schedule:** weekends summer and fall months; write for up-to-date information and fares. **Location:** Nelsonville is in southeastern Ohio on US-33, 67 miles from Columbus. **Of special note:** the beautiful, old-time station, not as old as it looks.

Cuyahoga Valley Line

A vintage train ride into the past

Riding the rails in Ohio's Cuyahoga Valley is more than a vintage train trip into the past. It is the opportunity to journey fifty-five miles through the beautiful Cuyahoga Valley from Independence to Akron, with a midway stop at the restored Western Reserve Village of Hale Farm.

A living museum, Hale Farm and Village depicts rural life in Ohio in the mid-1800s. Farmers, carpenters, blacksmiths, glass blowers, potters, spinners, and weavers ply their trades. Visitors tour restored homes and buildings, and a museum gift shop sells indigenous handcrafted items.

At the end of the line in Akron, a bus meets the train to take passengers to one of the following places during their three-hour stopover: Quaker Square, where former mills and silos of the original Quaker Oats factory have been converted to thirty-five unique shops and restaurants; the Akron Art Museum, which houses a fine collection of twentieth-century American art; Stan Hywet Hall and Gardens, the magnificent Tudor-revival mansion built by the founder of Goodyear; and the Akron Zoo.

In operation for over ten years, the Cuyahoga Valley Line was formed in 1975. The line's locomotive stands eighteen feet high, is more than eighty-one feet long, and, fully loaded, carries eighteen tons of coal and 12,000 gallons of water. Known as a Mikado, this type was originally built for Nippon Railway in 1897. The Cuyahoga's 2-8-2 was once used as the backup engine for Harry Truman's whistle-stop campaign.

The railroad offers first-class service on its beautifully restored car, the Mt. Baxter. Built by the Pullman Company in 1924, it was modernized in 1939. Recently, this combination Pullman-parlor car, with its moss green and gilt interior, was painstakingly restored to its 1939 appearance. To add to the feeling that passengers have stepped back in time, the car features a sound system that envelopes them in the music of the 30s and 40s.

Next to the Hilton Hotel complex and Quaker Oats factory in Akron, there are seven rail passenger cars: two from the Broadway Limited, one from the Jeffersonian, one from the General. There is also one of the world's largest model railroads, with a mile of track and 1,500 cars and locomotives.

Cuyahoga Valley Line, operating railroad of the Cuyahoga Valley Preservation and Scenic Railway Association, P.O. Box 502, Sagamore Hill, Ohio 44067; (216) 468-0797. A 55-mile scenic trip to Quaker Square in Akron and the 19th-century Jonathan Hale Farm and Village. **Schedule:** Saturdays only, mid-June to mid-Oct, except Labor Day, leaving approx. 11 A.M. and returning 5:30 P.M. Leaves passengers at Hale Farm at noon, and picks up at 4:30 P.M. Arrives Quaker Sq. 12:45 and leaves 4 P.M. for return trip. **Fares:** Hale Farm $11.95, children $7.95; Quaker Sq. $17.95, children $9.95; Hale Farm to Quaker Sq. $9.95, children $5.95. **Location:** depot is in Independence, Ohio, a suburb of Cleveland near Rocks Side and Canal Road. **Of special note:** Depot Restaurant at Quaker Sq. is filled with railroad memorabilia, an 1886 Telegraph Office, and a Yard Master's office.

Left, Mikado No. 4070 arriving at the Akron yards to turn on the wye. Photograph Ron Johnson. Right, the main feature of Akron's Quaker Square is the transformed Quaker Oats cereal factory, now a Hilton Inn—grain silos, rail lines, and all.

Overleaf, steaming alongside the Cuyahoga River all the way to Akron. Photograph David Post.

French Lick, West Baden & Southern Railway

A re-creation of a 1920s branch line

Starting up in 1978, the French Lick, West Baden & Southern Railway was the name chosen for the operating segment of the Indiana Railway Museum. The twenty-five-year-old museum, a nonprofit organization, secures, preserves, restores, displays, and operates historic railway equipment. It operates out of the 1907 limestone Monon Passenger Station through the generosity of the French Lick Springs Hotel.

French Lick, well known for its mineral springs, was commercially developed during the nineteenth century, when the spring water was bottled and sold under the name "Pluto Water." Grand hotels were built in French Lick and West Baden, and by the turn of the century the area was a popular health resort.

Today, a twenty-mile round-trip train ride from French Lick to Cuzco recreates a 1920s branch-line passenger

train that operated from French Lick. The train wends its way through part of the Hoosier National Forest, traverses wooded Indiana limestone country, and passes through one of the state's longest railway tunnels, the 2,200-foot-long Burton Tunnel. The train is made up of passenger cars from three railroads: the Rock Island, the Milwaukee, and the Erie.

The museum also operates a 1925 Bald-

Above left, the 1912 Pullman car, Birmingham, parked on the private car siding.
Above, a 1925 Baldwin 2-6-0 en route from French Lick to Cuzco.
Left, the station, built in 1907 from Indiana limestone.

win steam engine from the Mobile & Gulf Railroad and two Alco diesel locomotives from the Algers Winslow & Western Railroad. It has recently restored an electric street-car system from the early 1900s.

Museum member David McClure now owns the *Birmingham,* formerly the private car of the president of the Seaboard Air Line Railway. In 1983, it was carried by Amtrak on a main-line excursion to New York City, Boston, and Montreal. The car is believed to be the first private car pulled by Amtrak to carry the reporting marks of a tourist railroad. The car, lettered French Lick, West Baden & Southern, sported number 14. Riding

on the high iron at ninety miles an hour, the *Birmingham* made a successful trip. Its owner is planning other excursions.

French Lick, West Baden & Southern Railway, P.O. Box 150, French Lick, Indiana 47432; (812) 936-2405. Operating railroad of the Indiana Railway Museum; a 1¾ hour, 20-mile round trip between the resort town of French Lick and Cuzco, Indiana. **Schedule:** open Saturdays and Sundays, April through November, and Memorial Day, July 14th, and Labor Day. Trains depart the old Monon Railroad station in French Lick at 10 A.M., 1 P.M., 4 P.M. EST (note that Indiana does not observe Daylight Saving Time). **Fare:** adults $6; children $3; special group rates. **Location:** on Route 56 off US-150, south of Indianapolis. **Of special note:** the equipment of the Indiana Railway Museum in French Lick.

Boone & Scenic Valley Railroad

The folks in Boone, Iowa, have a hobby, railroading, and a motto, "people make it happen." The explosive energy generated when a whole community pulls together can accomplish miracles. Given the number of years it usually takes to develop an operating railroad, imagine chartering a railroad in the spring, buying eleven miles of abandoned line in the summer, running the first train in the fall, and paying for it all before Christmas.

That was the scenario in 1983 when people in Boone formed the Boone Railroad Historical Society to save, preserve, restore, and maintain vintage railroad equipment and memorabilia. Boone has a strong railroad heritage—many townspeople are active and retired employees of the Chicago and Northwestern Rail-

road and the Fort Dodge, Des Moines & Southern Railroad—so the town called on the wealth of knowledge available locally. Volunteers even purchased some passenger cars—ex-Rock Island, and Chicago & South Shore cars are now in service. In the second year of operation, 47,000 passengers enjoyed the scenic ride.

The plan is to bring back all three types of motive power—steam, electric, and diesel. The Society started with a diesel locomotive and has revived some electric trolleys. It is looking for the ideal specimen of steam. In the meantime, Boone has built a new station in the tradition of

A town of miracle workers

the grand old ones from the turn of the century.

The Boone & Scenic Valley Railroad is the operating division of the Historical Society, and it has a wonderful piece of the old Fort Dodge, Des Moines & Southern track on which to operate. There are magnificent views of the Des Moines River valley, numerous cuts and fills along the line to add spice, and various bridges, including the High Bridge, 800 feet long and 156 feet above the valley floor. Riders are flocking to the line by the thousands to turn back the hands of time, if only for a day.

Boone & Scenic Valley Railroad, P.O. Box 603, Boone, Iowa 50036; (515) 432-4249. A 10½ mile roundtrip through the Des Moines River Valley in Iowa's heartland. **Schedule:** weekdays at 11 A.M.; weekends, rain or shine, from Memorial Day to Oct. 28, incl. holidays; 4 trips daily, 11 A.M., 1, 3, 5 P.M. **Fares:** $6, children half; charters. **Location:** 40 miles northwest of Des Moines—take I-35 to Ames and US-30 west to Boone, go north on Story Street to 10th Street and west to Division Street. **Special note:** the highest single-track interurban bridge in the U.S.

Mid-Continent Railway

The American dream came true in the age of steam, when the great and powerful traveled in elegant coaches of gleaming brass and polished mahogany, pulled by one of man's most glorious creations—the steam locomotive. But steam eventually gave way to progress and became a quaint vestige that had little to do with the mainstream of transportation. Most of the steam engines were put to the torch, as were the cars, stations, and in many cases, whole railroads.

Back in 1959, the Mid-Continent Railway Historical Society consisted of just four members and an idea: to own and operate a steam railroad. Railroading experience was gained through an agreement with the five-mile Hillsboro & Northeastern Railway, when the first runs of the Mid-Continent rolled along behind a gasoline, not a steam, locomotive.

A meticulous collection of the steam era

Still interested in its own railroad line, the Wisconsin group examined the weedy right-of-way of a 4½-mile branch line of the Chicago & North Western at North Freedom. The branch, listed in the timetable as the Rattlesnake Line, had been laid in 1903 to serve iron-ore mines but was abandoned in 1962. The Society floated bonds, bought the line, and by May, 1963, railroad enthusiasts began the meticulous re-creation of the steam era at North Freedom. Beginning with a single track, the amateur railroaders laid new ties, spiked down rails, and brought

Left, Western Coal & Coke No. 1 heads toward Quartzite Lake through an autumn landscape. Right, an old Omaha hogger, the late Harold Van Horn, at the throttle of Warren and Quachita Valley No. 1. Photographs Geoffrey Blaesing.

Above, night-time lighting delineates the detail on a Chicago & North Western 4-6-0. *Left,* another look at Western Coal & Coke No. 1, this time leading a triple header. *Right,* the line's oldest engine, an 1884 Dardanelle and Russellville Mogul atop the Baraboo River bridge. Photographs Geoffrey Blaesing.

in the first cars. Since then, they have constructed buildings and moved old ones to North Freedom and purchased rail equipment of all kinds. Other equipment has been donated.

By June, 1963, steam was running again. Society members overcame problems as they learned how to handle coal shovels, solve lubrication mysteries, and fix leaks here and there—all genuine short-line railroading problems. Railroaders, retired and active, pitched in to help. And the work continues. The volunteers—lawyers, civil engineers, doctors, and students among them—change garb to keep the re-created 1910 repair shop humming, sell tickets in the 1895 depot, and act as conductors and brakemen.

The search for steam has brought to North Freedom a locomotive collection of distinction. Examples of early turn-of-the-century types include a Baldwin 4-6-0 from Chicago & North Western, which handled the first runs; a Baldwin 2-6-0 Mogul that was built for the New Orleans and Northeastern Railway; and two more ten-wheeler 4-6-0s—a 1906 Baldwin from Arkansas and a 1913 Montreal Locomotive Works beauty from Alberta. Fully reconditioned and cared for with love and dedication, they have been welded, refitted, and polished under the guidance of professional railroaders and state inspectors.

Mid-Continent Railway, North Freedom, Wisconsin 53951; (608) 522-4261. Operating railroad of the Mid-Continent Railway Historical Society. A 9-mile, 50-minute trip through the scenic Baraboo River valley. **Schedule:** 4 trips daily, rain or shine, from mid-May through Labor Day weekend; weekends only through 2nd weekend in October. Trains depart from depot at foot of Walnut Street at 11 A.M. and 1, 2:30, and 4 P.M. **Fares:** $6; children half; group rates. **Location:** northwest of Madison off Route 136 west of US-12. **Of special note:** the Railway Museum, with a dozen locomotives on display.

Algoma Central Railway

One of the last remaining old-time railroads that still handles passengers as well as freight, the Algoma Central was built to transport the wealth from Canada's vast, resource-rich hinterland. Construction began in 1899 at Sault (pronounced "Soo") Ste. Marie in northwestern Ontario, and as Canada prospered from the timber and minerals found there, the railroad did too. Passengers still see great names of industry on the box cars that are shunted about the freight yards: Abitibi, Union Carbide, Domtar, Weyerhaeuser, Algoma Steel.

More successful today than ever, the railroad maintains 325 miles of main-line track in perfect condition. The line stretches north into virgin wilderness that

Crossing the Bellevue Valley trestle, 100 feet high and 810 feet long.

A wilderness experience

is accessible only by train. The lakes, streams, canyons, mountains, and gorges attract so many thousands of visitors each season that the railroad built a special passenger terminal in 1974.

The Algoma provides passengers with a choice of three rides: a two-day tour of the line "north to the end of the steel"; a one-day tour of the thrilling Agawa Canyon; and a one-day winter trip on the Snow Train, which the railroad calls "a wilderness experience."

TOUR OF THE LINE

A 300-mile roundtrip tour of the entire line begins at Sault Ste. Marie and ends at Hearst, Ontario, a French Canadian logging town called the "Moose Capital of Canada" and the northern terminus of the railroad. Passengers eat dinner and spend the night in Hearst and return the next day. The twenty-car train, pulled by four diesel locomotives that are brightly painted in the railroad's maroon and gray livery, departs at 8:30 A.M. The train is only twenty miles out when it crosses the first of two major trestles on the line. The first trestle, 100 feet high and 810 feet long, provides a breathtaking view of Bellevue Valley. Seventy-two miles farther along, an even larger trestle crosses the Montreal River. This trestle, 130 feet high and 1,550 feet long, is one of the longest in Canada. The line's ultimate thrill is yet to come, though. Some 22 miles farther on, the track snakes through the Agawa River Canyon, with sheer walls that at some points are only fifty feet apart. The train turns around in Hearst on the world's largest "wye," which is created when the track intersects with the northern line of the Canadian National Railway. Theoretically, a train 294 miles long could be turned here.

AGAWA CANYON TOUR

The main features of the line—the two dramatic trestles and the thrilling Agawa Canyon—can be experienced on this one-day tour that leaves at 8:00 A.M. and arrives back at 4:30 P.M.

THE SNOW TRAIN

Every weekend from December 29 through March 24, the train makes a 120-mile trip through the northern countryside, which forty-degrees-below-zero-Fahrenheit temperatures have transformed into a true winter wonderland of powdery snow and ice as clear as crystal. The train leaves at 8:30 A.M. and arrives back in Sault Ste. Marie at 4:30 P.M. Because of low temperatures and snow accumulation, the train does not make a stopover before returning.

DINING-CAR FACILITIES are available on all trains immediately upon boarding at Sault Ste. Marie. Service is continuous until 3:45 P.M. and includes full breakfast, hot and cold lunch, confectionery, and cold drinks. Take-out box lunches are also available.

Algoma Central Railway, 129 Bay Street, Sault Ste. Marie 26, Ontario, Canada P6A 5P6; (705) 254-4331. One and 2-day trips through Ontario wilderness in modern passenger coaches. **Schedule:** Tour of the line and Agawa Canyon daily from early June to mid-Oct. Times given in the text are Eastern Daylight. Tour of the line weekends only Jan. 1 to May 25 and mid-Oct. to Dec. 31. Snow train weekends only. **Fares:** (Canadian funds) Tour of the Line $65, lodging in Hearst extra, reservations required (Northern Season's Motel (705) 362-4281); Agawa Canyon $30; Snow Train $30; children half. **Location:** Sault Ste. Marie is on the isthmus between Lake Superior and Lake Huron on the Michigan border very near Duluth, Minn. Driving, the Trans-Canada Hwy goes through from Sudbury; by train, VIA rail lines go through on the way west. **Of special note:** from 1918 to 1923, Canada's most famous artists, the Group of Seven, painted the Algoma area from a boxcar outfitted into a cabin, shunted to various sidings about the area.

Royal Hudson Steam Train

Left, the steel-clad, gleaming locomotive runs past one of the many marinas that dot Howe Sound. Photograph Ron Johnson. Below, King George VI and Queen Elizabeth in 1939 on the observation platform of the Royal Train. Photograph Vancouver Public Library.

In 1939 the Canadian Pacific Railway had the honor of pulling the Royal Train that took King George VI and Queen Elizabeth on a 3,224-mile tour of Canada, from Quebec City in the east to Vancouver on the west coast. The steam locomotive selected for the task was number 2850, a Hudson 4-6-4 built for the Canadian Pacific in the 1930s by the Montreal Locomotive Works.

Developed by the New York Central Railroad, and named after the Hudson River, along which its tracks ran, the Hudsons were distinguished by their 4-6-4 wheel arrangement. This allowed for a larger firebox than those used on earlier locomotives, resulting in more superheated steam at a higher boiler pressure. With 75-inch drivers, the locomotives could run faster and pull heavier trains.

The 2850, specially painted in silver and blue, steamed across Canada through twenty-five changes of crew without a single engine failure, while the king, an ardent railway buff, rode in the cab at every opportunity. Following this stalwart performance, King George was so impressed that he dubbed the locomotive "Royal." Henceforth, all CPR Hudson passenger locomotives had crowns placed on the running boards and were known as Royal Hudsons. The 2850 went on to be exhibited at the 1939 New York World's Fair.

The 2860, built in 1940 for use in British Columbia, was the first engine built as a Royal Hudson. From 1940 to 1956, she ran through the canyons and tunnels between Vancouver and Revelstoke, hauling the great transcontinental passenger trains. But technology caught up with her. Diesels replaced steam engines

The engine that captured the heart of a king

Painted in the traditional Canadian Pacific colors, black and tuscan red, the Royal Hudson skirts along the water for most of the distance, affording an exciting variety of seascapes, and an occasional landscape. Photographs Tourism B.C.

and most Royal Hudsons, including 2860, were retired to the scrap heap and left to rust.

Over the years, there were a number of aborted efforts to resurrect 2860, but it wasn't until 1973 that the Royal Hudson saw hope for a new life. The government of British Columbia decided to buy and restore her.

The major tasks in preparing the 2860 to run again were rebuilding her boiler and making a new jacket of stainless steel. New boiler tubes and new superheater units had to be installed; new brasses for the side rods had to be cast. On June 20, 1974, one of the largest steam locomotives in regular passenger service on the North American continent started a new career.

Each summer, from mid-May to mid-September, the Royal Hudson hauls eleven ex-CPR 1940s passenger coaches, a baggage car, and a dining car through some of the most picturesque mountain and ocean scenery in the Pacific Northwest. The eighty-mile journey, from North Vancouver to Squamish and back, takes 800 passengers along spectacular Howe Sound, over trestles, and through the tunnels of the British Columbia Railway.

To make the trip even more memorable, passengers can go one way by sea on the *M.V. Britannia,* which makes a parallel journey beside the towering cliffs of the sound. From the promenade deck passengers can spot the Royal Hudson as it winds its way along the water's edge.

Royal Hudson Steam Train, c/o B.C. Railway, 1311 First Street, North Vancouver, B.C., Canada V7P 1A7; (604) 987-5211 for reservations (required); (604) 689-8687 for information; regularly scheduled steam excursions pulled by ex-CPR Royal Hudson 2860, operated by the provincial Ministry of Tourism over the tracks of the British Columbia Railway. A 40-mile trip from North Vancouver along stunning seacoast to Squamish at the head of Howe Sound; choice of round trip by train or one way by train and one way by equally delightful boat ride. **Schedule:** mid-May through mid-Sept. 5 days a week, Wednesday through Sunday and certain holiday Mondays. Train departs from B.C. Railway terminal at 1311 West 1st Street, North Vancouver at 10:30 A.M., returning at 3:55 P.M. The boat, MV Britannia, departs from Harbour Ferries at foot of Denman Street (north end) in Vancouver at 9:30 A.M. and returns at 4:30 P.M. Free shuttle from train to dock and vice versa to collect automobiles. **Fares:** $12 round trip by train and $34 round trip by train and boat; less for children and seniors. **Location:** train station is on right at north end of Lions Gate suspension bridge, coming through Stanley Park from Vancouver. **Of special note:** Business Coach charters, complete train charters, and group bookings.

British Columbia Railway

Sightseeing beyond one's wildest dreams

On most maps of British Columbia, a thin black line twists and winds its way northward from Vancouver to the oil-rich Peace River country in the northeastern corner of the province. For 729 miles, the line passes through some of the most stunningly beautiful areas on the North American continent: Howe Sound, Cheakamus Canyon, Anderson and Seton lakes, which are set like jewels amid towering mountains, the wild loneliness of the south Cariboo, Williams Lake, and Quesnel cattle country, the fantastic Rocky Mountain trench, and finally, the gentle rolling hills of the Peace River country.

There was a time when people thought that this thin black line—now called the British Columbia Railway—should have been "the thin red line." The Provincial government founded the line in 1912 as the *Pacific Great Eastern Railway*. Year after year staggering deficits piled up, and the line earned such names as Provincial Government Expense, Promotors Get Everything, Please Go Easy, Past

God's Endurance, and many other unflattering plays upon the initials P.G.E. Taxpayers even saw a symbol in the twisting and turning of the tracks, saying that the original builders were so crooked that they couldn't bring themselves to order straight trackage.

Built in the hopes of stimulating commercial development, the railroad began nowhere and went nowhere for a good part of its life. This impracticality only made the line more attractive to its passengers, who loved to ride its motley collection of old cars into the vast, remote wilderness of British Columbia. Passengers enjoyed sight-seeing beyond their wildest dreams, and fan clubs boasted continent-wide memberships. Thousands of people headed north from American points just to travel on the P.G.E., and the *Saturday Evening Post* and other magazines waxed eloquent over the unique railroad.

Today nothing has changed except the equipment and service: sleek, stainless-steel Budd diesel railcars are pleasantly comfortable, and meals are served at your seat by stewards. The romance of steam may be gone, but the untamed wilderness is still breathtaking.

B.C. Rail Ltd., Passenger Sales & Service, P.O. Box 8770, Vancouver, British Columbia, Canada V6B 4X6; (604) 984-5246. One and 2-day rail trips through the incredibly scenic Canadian province. **Schedule:** (for Cariboo Class, including meals) 1-day to Lillooet, 157 miles, leaving Sun., Wed., Fri. at 7 A.M., arriving noon, and leaving 3 P.M. for arrival North Van. depot 8:15 P.M. Same train goes on to Prince George, arriving 8:15 P.M. 462 miles distance. Return to Van. Mon., Thur., Sat., leaving 7 A.M. arriving 8:15 P.M., or connect with VIA (Canadian National Railway line) to Prince Rupert or Edmonton and all points east. There is a coach service 7 days a week to Lillooet only, no meals, leaving and returning same times as above. **Fares:** coach to Lillooet, each way, $18.15; to Prince George $52.25; children 5–11 half, 2–4 quarter. Surcharge for Cariboo Class in separate car with kitchen, bar, and spacious seating: return to Lillooet or one-way to Prince George $23 (same for children). Coach passengers may purchase light snacks from steward on board. **Location:** same as Royal Hudson.

Left, although self-propelled, the diesel rail cars are often coupled together into trains. Photograph Ron Johnson. Right, photograph Tourism B.C.

Lake Whatcom Railway

In 1959, when Frank E. Culp was a nineteen-year-old college student, railroads were getting rid of their steam engines. There was also talk about lines back East like the Strasburg that were putting together tourist trains and making a go of it. That year a Northern Pacific engine came up for sale for $2,500.

Frank always wanted to go into his own business and had put $150 aside. He tried raising the rest. Ed Campbell, president of the North Western Glass Company and a lover of "steam," came up with an offer Frank couldn't refuse. He offered to buy the 0-6-0 switcher and hold it until Frank could afford to buy it

back. In 1963, when he went to work as a civil engineer for Northern Pacific, Frank redeemed the engine.

Frank then added two 1910–1912 vintage Northern Pacific Pullman green coaches with red velvet seats to the engine. He could only afford one of the parlor cars, but his parents lent him $1,800 to buy the second. He stored his

*Above, star of the show, No. 1070 was built around 1906. **Right,** Santa Claus and Christmas carols herald the season.*

A train ride as it was 50 years ago

engine and rolling stock in search of a railroad in towns near Seattle.

In 1972, after a railroad merger, Frank was able to buy a scenic four-mile section of the old Northern Pacific line that had run from Seattle to Bellingham since 1902. With the help of his brother, Bob, and some dedicated volunteers, he began operating the train on a schedule that has never slipped since 1972.

The Lake Whatcom Railway is unique among the far-western steam railroads of the 1980s because it is not operated as a museum, as an amusement ride, or as a sideline to anything else. People simply experience a train ride as it was fifty years ago. The train passes lakes, beaver lodges, and a small village as it winds its way through the forested foothills of Washington's Cascade Mountains.

Midway through the trip, the train moves onto a siding, and passengers are invited into the cab of the old steam engine for a tour. In the summer, a member of the train crew will often take passengers for a ride on an old hand pump car (the passengers have to do the pumping). Passengers are also often invited to ride on one of the railroad's speeders. On the Lake Whatcom Railway, a fantasy can come true—trains can be chartered anytime for $500.

Lake Whatcom Railway, P.O. Box 91, Acme, Washington 98220; (206) 595-2218. A 1 hour nostalgic steam trip through the forests and farmlands of northwestern Washington. **Schedule:** Saturdays and Tuesdays, June through August, leaving Wickersham Junction at noon and 2 P.M. **Fares:** $6, children under 17, $3; group rates for whole coach, parlor car, or whole train, any day. **Location:** east of Bellingham; from south on I-5, take exit 240; drive 5 miles east to Sedro Woolley and north on Route 9 for 11 miles to Wickersham; from north on I-5 exit at Mt. Baker highway and drive east to Deming and south to Wickersham on Route 9—watch for railway sign on left, very visible.

Puget Sound and Snoqualmie Valley Railroad

A breathtaking view of the valley

*Other attractions are the Victorian depot, the Mallet steam engine (photographs Dan Olah), and the ex-Union Pacific observation car, **below** (photograph Maynard Laing).*

Just thirty miles east of Seattle, Washington, the Puget Sound and Snoqualmie Valley Railroad carries passengers on a scenic ten-mile round trip through a valley nestled in the Cascade foothills. The seventy-minute journey takes riders past lush farms beneath beautiful Mount Si and through thick stands of evergreens between the towns of Snoqualmie and North Bend. The train then proceeds to spectacular Snoqualmie Falls (268 feet high) for a breathtaking view of the lower valley.

The railroad is owned and operated by the Puget Sound Railway Historical Association, a nonprofit, all-volunteer organization dedicated to the preservation and operation of steam, electric, diesel, and logging railroad equipment. Founded in 1957, the Association's collection has grown from one passenger car to more than ninety pieces of equipment: steam locomotives, diesels, streetcars, a variety of passenger and freight cars, a rotary snowplow, steam cranes, and work equipment. At the present time, U.S. Plywood number 11, a 2-6-6-2 Mallet, is the only steam locomotive in service.

Built by Baldwin in 1926, it is one of the few operating Mallets in North America. Efforts are under way to restore two more steamers and return them to service.

The showplace and hub of the railroad is the restored depot in Snoqualmie, built in 1890 for the Seattle, Lake Shore and Eastern Railway. It is no wonder that the depot, with its distinctive cupola and round-ended waiting room, has been placed on the National Register of Historic Places. The Burlington Northern Railroad donated the depot, as well as three and a half miles of a former Northern Pacific branch line, to the Historical Association in 1977. The depot serves as the Association's base of operations and houses displays and a bookstore.

The last weekend in October brings a special run on the Haunted Train. Freshly pressed apple cider and doughnuts are served in the depot, and patrons in Halloween costumes ride for half fare. Santa trains run from the decorated Victorian depot for two weekends in December.

The Puget Sound Railway Historical Association, always happy to receive funds, suggests the following gifts for train afficionados: a membership in the association or a private charter of the train for a party or wedding.

Puget Sound & Snoqualmie Valley Railroad, P.O. Box 459, Snoqualmie, Washington 98065; (206) 746-4025. Operating railroad of the Puget Sound Railway Historical Association; a 10-mile trip through the valley over track dating back to 1880. **Schedule:** Sundays from April through Oct. and Saturdays from Memorial Day weekend through Sept.; 4 trains every 1½ hrs from 11:01 A.M. to 3:31 P.M.; extra train at 5:01 during high season from Snoqualmie only. **Fares:** steam train $5, seniors over 62, $4, children $3; diesel train or trolley $1 less; group rates. **Location:** may board at either of 2 depots, Snoqualmie or North Bend; on I-90 to or from Seattle, exit 31 for North Bend or exit 27 for Snoqualmie. **Of special note:** the 1890 Snoqualmie depot donated by Burlington Northern.

Overleaf, a 1922 Baldwin Mikado crossing the Snoqualmie River bridge, with Mt. Si in the distance. Photograph Maynard Laing.

Lahaina-Kaanapali & Pacific

The blue Pacific, humpback whales, and *sugar* *cane*

Nicknamed "The Sugar Cane Train," the Lahaina-Kaanapali & Pacific Railroad travels through breathtaking Maui past swaying sugar cane, clay-colored foothills, and spectacular ocean views. On a twelve-mile trip into the past, riders experience turn-of-the-century plantation life. A singing conductor, complete with ukulele, serenades tourists with an entertaining account of the region's sights and history. Pioneer Mill, Ltd., which still grows sugar cane, built the original railroad bed and once used the train to transport sugar workers into the fields and cane to nearby mills.

From 1882 to the end of the 1952 sugar cane season, the Pioneer Mill had a 30-inch narrow-gauge railroad. Then, the company removed the rails and widened and rebuilt most of the main-line roadbed to handle the huge cane trucks that replaced the train.

A. W. "Mac" McKelvey is responsible for bringing the Sugar Cane Train back. A fighter pilot and test pilot in the Pacific during World War II, McKelvey returned to the islands in 1962. On a trip to Lahaina, he began to dream about reviving the old railroad, at least the part between Lahaina and the resort area of Kaanapali. With backing from the operators of Sea Life Park Aquarium on Oahu, he brought the Lahaina-Kaanapali & Pacific Railroad into being.

Custom-built in Pennsylvania in 1969, the train's three coaches were patterned after the Kalakaua coaches used on the big island's Hawaii Railway. Coaches of this style were made famous in 1883, when King Kalakaua rode in one on his way to the dedication of a statue of Kamehameha I. Two steam engines, restored to resemble the locomotives used in Hawaii at the turn of the century, pull the coaches.

In 1972, the new operation went into bankruptcy and closed down. Willis B. Kyle, who owns several other short lines and whose business has always been railroading, purchased the entire Lahaina Kaanapali & Pacific Railroad in 1973. It has been running ever since. The line is the only railroad operating in Hawaii, and it gives passengers a chance to relive the days of the Kahului & Wailuku, the Hawaii railway that played a big part in developing the fiftieth state.

The ride between the lusty old whaling town of Lahaina and the picturesque resort area of Kaanapali is a magnificent sight-seeing adventure. The blue Pacific, the green cane fields, and the islands in the distance create a dazzling panorama. Occasionally, passengers spot humpback whales off Lahaina harbor or glimpse an afternoon rainbow in the valleys of the West Maui Mountains.

ailroad

Above, the restored Anaka locomotive arrived in Lahaina after tryouts on the East Broad Top Narrow-Gauge Railroad in Pennsylvania.

Lahaina-Kaanapali & Pacific Railroad, P.O. Box 816, Lahaina, Maui, Hawaii 96761; (808) 667-6851. Nicknamed The Sugar Cane Train, the route winds through fields of sugar cane between the historic whaling town of Lahaina and the resort area of Kaanapali, with its spectacular ocean views, for a 12-mile, 1 hour trip. **Schedule:** daily, year-round, from 9:30 A.M. to 4:10 P.M. **Fares:** $7, children half. Special tour packages include lunch, museums, and old ship tour, glassbottom boat trip over coral reefs, jitney pass, etc. **Location:** board the train at 3 locations—Puukolii Platform across from the Kaanapali airstrip at the Kaanapali resort; Kaanapali Station across from the Maui Eldorado at Kaanapali resort; Lahaina Station on Honoapiilani Hwy 1½ blocks north of Lahainaluna Road. **Of special note:** rebuilt steam engines "Anaka" and "Myrtle," both 2-4-0 Porters built in 1943.

The railroad's advertising is patterned after an 1869 Union Pacific poster, now a collector's item.

California Western Railroad

31 bridges, 2 tunnels, and towering redwoods

The best-known and most-traveled tourist railroad on the West Coast has to be the California Western, popularly known as the Skunk Railroad.

Begun in 1885 as a logging railroad, its construction proceeded only as fast as the giant redwood trees could be logged. By 1887, the railroad, which runs inland from Fort Bragg on California's north coast, was 6.6 miles long. A 1,122-foot-long tunnel extended the line to ten miles by 1898. Winding up slopes and around curves the whole distance, it reached 27.8 miles by 1910. The planned eastern terminus was five miles farther inland at Willits, where the line would connect with the Northwestern Pacific track creeping north from San Francisco. But the terrain was so mountainous that it took twelve miles of track to complete the line by 1911.

Passenger service opened in 1911 and was such a success that tourist excursions have continued ever since. The line got a big boost when the Northwestern Pacific finally reached Willits in 1913, providing transcontinental connections for both passengers and freight on the little shortline railroad.

With thirty-one bridges, two tunnels, towering redwoods, and green meadows carpeted in wild flowers, the year-round, three-hour ride is as exciting and scenic today as it ever was. In fact, there are

so many riders that it is a good idea to reserve tickets immediately upon arrival in either Willits or Fort Bragg and then wait your turn.

Three kinds of motive power are now in ·use: a Baldwin 2-8-2 Mikado steam engine running several days a week, Baldwin road switcher logging diesels, and diesel rail buses by various makers. The buses were introduced in 1925 to handle increased passenger traffic, and the first one, made by Mack Truck, emitted such a cloud of fumes as it ran back and forth that passengers dubbed it "the skunk." Although fumes are not a problem anymore, the nickname stuck and the railroad has been known affectionately as The Skunk ever since.

Both Willits, on Highway 101, and Fort Bragg, on the Pacific, have interesting dining, shopping, and recreation facilities. On the coast, whale watching is especially popular here in the heart of Mendocino county.

California Western Railroad, P.O. Box 907, Fort Bragg, California 95437; (707) 964-6371. A scenic 40-mile trip through the Redwoods behind steam, diesel, or railcar, from Fort Bragg on the Pacific and Willits on US-101, or half-way from either direction to Northspur and back. **Schedule:** daily during summers—3rd Sat. in June to 2nd Sat. in Sept.; daily winter diesel car service thereafter except Thanksgiving, Christmas, and New Year's Day; morning departure, returning in afternoon. In summer 3-hour roundtrip to Northspur departs in morning, returning for lunch. **Fares:** Fort Bragg-Willits, round trip $16, one way $12, children half; return to Northspur $12, children $7. **Location:** Fort Bragg is on the Pacific Coast Hwy north of San Francisco, and Willits is inland on US-101. **Of special note:** the steam train, but it only runs on certain days.

Above left, passengers on the open observation car get the best look at the stately redwoods that line the route. Right, diesel crossing one of the 31 bridges.

Roaring Camp & Big Trees Narrow-Gauge Railroad

Restored by a man with a childhood passion for trains

Left, now a classic, this photograph shows the Shay locomotive crossing over its own caboose, a feat not many railroads can do. Right, Indian Creek trestle, which forms a long horseshoe loop through the forest.

The restoration of the Roaring Camp & Big Trees grizzly bear route through California's monumental redwoods is the dream-come-true of Norman and Georgiana Clark. Back in 1958, with $25 in his pocket and a childhood passion for trains, Clark got a ninety-nine-year lease to restore passenger train service. With the help of friends, backers, and well-thumbed old train manuals, Clark designed, rebuilt, and engineered the rail line, which was originally completed in 1879. It carried passengers from Santa Cruz to Felton and was later extended across the mountains from San Jose to Alameda. Despite a brief shutdown after the earthquake of 1906, as many as a dozen steam passenger trains were stopping at Felton and Roaring Camp. But a winter storm damaged the line in 1940, and it was abandoned except for a small branch line—until Clark rescued it.

Passengers approach the steam train by walking across an old covered bridge to the Roaring Camp depot, which is located on 179 acres of unspoiled land timbered with redwood, madrone, and oak. The cluster of buildings looks like an 1880's town and includes a general store, the depot, and a caboose-turned-saloon that serves soft drinks. Isaac Graham, the trapper-sawmill operator-revolutionary nephew of Daniel Boone, established one of America's first settlements on this site.

On the hour-long excursion to Bear Mountain, over the steepest grades in North America, breathtaking forests of giant redwoods tower hundreds of feet over the train. Passing through such station points as Big Trees, Indian Creek, Grizzly Flats, and Deer Valley, the train crosses spectacular trestles that span virgin redwood-forested canyons. At Bear Mountain, passengers can stop at the summit to picnic and hike and catch a later train back.

For passengers returning from Bear Mountain to Roaring Camp, a delicious chuckwagon barbecue lunch, featuring charcoal broiled steaks, is served beneath the trees. The railroad's famous moonlight steam-train parties include the steam-train excursion, a chuckwagon dinner, old-time country music, and dancing under the stars.

Roaring Camp & Big Trees Narrow-Gauge Railroad, Felton, California 95018; (408) 335-4484. An hour-long excursion pulled by 1890's engines over spectacular wooden trestles through thousand-year-old redwood forests. **Schedule:** one train daily at noon year-round; from June 2 to Sept. 3 increased to 5 trains leaving every 75 minutes from 11 A.M. on. Moonlight steam train party with barbeque, music, dancing on Sat. evenings June through Oct. **Fares:** $8.75, children $5.75. **Location:** a few miles north of Santa Cruz on Route 9 just south of Felton, on Graham Hill road. **Of special note:** old-time country music, 1880s general store.

Overleaf, rounding Schoolhouse Curve in Roaring Camp Meadow, on the way back to the depot.

Sierra Railway

The railroad Hollywood made famous

Owned by the state of California, and operating as the Sierra Railway over Sierra Railroad (freight) trackage, the trains and the historic twenty-six-acre Jamestown complex are operated by the state of California as a non-profit corporation that is dedicated to the preservation of California railroading. Built to connect the mines and lumber mills of Tuolumne county with the rest of the world, the Sierra Railway has served as a vital lifeline through California's Mother Lode country since 1897.

The Mother Lode Cannonball offers a twelve-mile, one-hour journey from the depot at Jamestown to Chinese and return. The train travels along scenic Woods Creek, said to have produced more gold than any other stream of its size in California, and climbs up the steep oak-

studded grade on the dramatic return to Jamestown.

The Wine and Cheese Zephyr, a special, runs on Saturdays in spring and fall (reservations required). Attendants serve California wines, cheese, fresh fruit, and sourdough bread. Strolling musicians add a festive note as the train winds its way through oak-covered hills.

A summer special, the Twilight Limited, runs on Saturday afternoons. Cocktails and snacks are served against a background of music. A hearty steak, complete with all the trimmings and served on the picnic green, awaits passengers upon their return.

The Jamestown complex includes the blacksmith shop, car shops, machine shop with overhead-belt power system, turntable and roundhouse, a variety of historic equipment, vintage rolling stock, and steam locomotives. More than a relic of the past, the facility is used today to restore and maintain the Sierra's trains.

Nearly 200 feature films, TV shows, and commercials have been filmed on the Sierra Railway, for this is "the railroad Hollywood made famous." Such fabled classics as *The Virginian* (1929) with Gary Cooper, *Dodge City* (1939) with Errol Flynn, *My Little Chickadee* (1940) with W.C. Fields, and the all-time favorite, *High Noon* (1952), with Gary Cooper all used the Sierra. Steam locomotive number 3, Hollywood's favorite, has become the most-photographed locomotive in the world.

Left, Mother Lode Cannonball steaming through the California foothills. Below, a special railfan outing pulled by No. 28, a 1922 Consolidation. Below left, old No. 3, built in 1891, has starred in 100 movies. Photographs Dexter Day.

Sierra Railway, c/o Railtown 1897 State Historic Park, P.O. Box 1250, Jamestown, California 95327; (209) 984-3953. Railway and historic 26-acre Jamestown facilities of roundhouse, shop, station, and yards. **Schedule:** weekends mid-April through Oct. 27 for most trips; Roundhouse Tour goes daily May 25 to Sept. 2. **Fares:** write for details of fares, trips, schedules. **Location:** 2 hours from San Francisco in the Gold Country at junction of Routes 108 and 49. **Of special note:** the Wine and Cheese Zephyr and the Twilight Limited.

When he was a boy in his native Switzerland, Rudy Stauffer heard tales of the Yosemite Mountain–Sugar Pine Railroad—tales of the enormous Shay locomotives that hauled great log trains over the mighty Sierra. He was determined to come to America to see the huge, geared engines for himself.

By the time of Stauffer's arrival in 1954, the narrow-gauge logging train had long been a casualty of the Great Depression. Stauffer opened a small motel

The Yosemite Mt

Below, the lovingly restored 82-ton Shay, standing at the Yosemite Mountain station. Right, the Shay on Slab Creek Loop. Photographs Joseph T. Bispo.

An immigrant's dream come true

Sugar Pine Railroad

near the former Madera Sugar Pine mill and contented himself with evening strolls along the weed-grown right-of-way of the abandoned Sugar Pine Railroad. But ten years later he learned that a Shay locomotive was up for sale and quickly bought it, along with fourteen cars, two old speeders, and twenty tons of spare parts. He trucked the cumbersome load piecemeal 200 miles to his property and set about the challenging task of re-creating a portion of the old Sugar Pine Railroad.

The railroad had flourished from 1899 to 1933, hauling logs high up in the Sierra Nevadas to the sawmill in Sugar Pine. Five wood-burning Shay engines hauled massive log trains to the mill over an extensive railroad network. During those years almost a billion-and-a-half board feet of lumber were shipped to the worldwide market. Rudy Stauffer's Shay was much like the original Madera Sugar Pine Company's engines.

A Michigan lumberman, Ephraim Shay, developed the Shay geared engine in the 1870s. Later, the Lima Locomotive Works of Lima, Ohio, began to manufacture the engine, which was used extensively on logging and mining railroads, where steep grades, sharp curves, and uncertain roadbeds were involved.

The Shay design was unique in several ways. It had a vertically mounted engine on the right side of the boiler, just ahead of the cab. To compensate for the weight and position of the engine, the boiler was set over to the left of center, giving the locomotive an odd, unbalanced appearance. The connecting rods from the cylinders were attached to a crankshaft that ran along the right side at wheel level. The crankshaft, in turn, was connected by a series of universal couplings, telescoping sleeves, and shafts to bevel gears

driving each wheel. So every wheel on a Shay was a driven wheel, providing maximum adhesion to the track.

Shays were manufactured in profuse variety between 1880 and 1945. They ranged in size from tiny two-cylinder models to huge mainline behemoths that weighed as much as 150 tons. So diverse was their design that among the 2,761 Shays that the Lima Locomotive Works turned out, it is hard to find any two engines that are exactly alike.

In many ways, the construction and maintenance of a Shay-powered railroad is more difficult in modern times than it was in the age of steam. Available spare parts and knowledgeable people grow more scarce with each passing year. Luckily, Rudy's son Max carries on the grand tradition of railroading.

Yosemite Mt. Sugar Pine Railroad, Yosemite Mountain, Fish Camp, California 93623; (209) 683-7273. A 4-mile logging train ride through scenic Sierra National Forest, past such points as Horse Shoe Curve, Honey Hill Junction, Cold Spring Crossing, Lewis Creek Canyon, Slab Creek picnic area. **Schedule:** weekends June 8 through Sept. 2 and May 25–27; 4 trains depart 10:30 A.M., noon, 1:30, 3:30 P.M. A Jenny railcar operates daily April 13 through Oct. 13 on days when steam train is not running. **Fares:** steam $5.75, children $3.75; Jenny $4.25, children $2.25. **Location:** near south entrance to Yosemite National Park on Route 41. **Of special note:** Narrow Gauge Inn and restaurant, Thornberry Museum.

Texas State Railroad

From left to right, engineer Roger Graham, hosteler Ken Perkins, and fireman M. D. Stokes keep their train running on time.

A 503-acre realm of the Iron Horse

Left, two of the line's roster of engines, beautifully restored and maintained in its own shops: an 1896 ten-wheeler, above, and a 1911 Pacific, below.

Operated by the Texas Parks and Wildlife Department, the Texas State Railroad is the nation's longest and narrowest state park. Located in piney woods in the heart of east Texas, it runs through Cherokee and Anderson counties, between the towns of Palestine and Rusk. Four veteran steam engines, powering gold, red, and black cars, travel 25-mile-long ribbons of steel past tributaries called Bowles, One-Arm, Beans, and Talles Creek—names of tribal chiefs. The Cherokees farmed this land long before the white man arrived.

The state prison system constructed the railroad at the turn of the century to haul iron ore to the prison-operated smelter and foundry at Rusk. When the foundry doubled in size, convicts extended the initial five miles of track. By 1909, the line ran between Palestine and Rusk, with a 1,100-foot bridge across the Neches River. The extension provided an added dividend—it linked communities with the Saint Louis-Southwestern Railroad at Rusk and the International and Great Northern Railroad at Palestine.

The smelters were shut down in 1913 because they were no longer profitable, but the state continued to operate the railroad at a heavy loss. After upgrading the tracks (with surplus eighty-pound rail that the army no longer needed for World War II) the state leased the line to the Texas and New Orleans Railroad, the Texas Southeastern, and, most recently, to the Missouri Pacific.

Beginning in 1969, the line lay dormant, allowing woodland creatures to get the upper hand. In 1972, however, the Texas Parks and Wildlife Department, determined to allow visitors to relive the "Golden Age of Steam," began to reclaim the facility. The state used convict labor again, this time for renovation.

A native stone Victorian-style depot at the Rusk end of the line houses a large maintenance shop where locomotives and passenger coaches are restored and tended to. The Victorian-style depot at the Palestine end of the line is constructed of wood. Sandwiches, snacks, drinks, ice cream, and souvenirs are readily available in each station and aboard the trains.

Thundering through deep forests and over twenty-four large wooden trestles, the train crosses over creeks and rivers. Deer, fox, raccoons, opossum, quail, and doves abound in this 503-acre realm of the majestic iron horse, which is a three-hour drive from both Dallas and Houston.

Texas State Railroad, P.O. Box 39, Rusk, Texas 75785; (214) 683-2561 or (800) 442-8951. Operating railroad in the State Historical Park of the Texas Parks and Wildlife Department, running 25 miles between Rusk and Palestine through forests and over trestles. The park offers many recreational facilities. **Schedule:** weekends mid-March through May; end-of-May to mid-August, Thursday to Monday (closed Tues. and Wed.); weekends last week in August to Nov. 10. One train a day from each depot leaves 11 A.M., arrives other depot 12:30, leaves 1:30 and arrives back at 3 P.M. Inquire about special evening runs from Rusk. **Fares:** $6 round trip, children $4. **Location:** in Anderson and Cherokee counties in east Texas, 3 hours drive from Dallas, Houston, Texarkana, or Waco, off US-84.

Cripple Creek & Victor Narrow-Gauge Railroad

An eighteen-year-old silence was broken by the shrill blast of a steam whistle in the summer of 1967, when the Cripple Creek railroad operated over the first 1,000 feet of its newly laid track. The last train had steamed out of the former gold-mining town in 1949, when the only mine still working dug up turquoise—not gold.

The founder of the new railroad was John Birmingham, a chemist in Boulder, the Colorado university town north of Denver. His father was an engineer on the Union Pacific, and John's dormant railroad mania bloomed when he heard about a steam engine for sale. He bought it, but it was a 4-foot, 8½-inch standard gauge, and it required a more expensive railroad than he could build. Besides, Colorado is narrow-gauge country. The economy of narrow gauge became more appealing when John found two more locomotives in Mexico. They were not built to the 3-foot width common in

Just about everybody loves a train

America, but to a 2-foot gauge common in Europe that had been introduced to Central and South America.

John decided on Cripple Creek to build the railroad, because he could lease the old roadbed of the defunct Midland Terminal railroad, and have room for yards, a station, and parking near the old Midland station, which is now a museum. Besides, Cripple Creek was coming back to life as a historic tourist area. Dorothy and Wayne Mackin had restored the Imperial Hotel and established a live theatre, and Cripple Creek was flourishing. The railroad was a perfect addition, since John had decided to carry tourists to generate the operating revenue that every railroad needs.

To carry passengers, cars were needed, but 2-foot gauge cars did not exist in America. Luckily, the Great Western, a small freight railroad with shops in Loveland, Colorado, was able to build two passenger cars while overhauling the two locomotives from Mexico.

Luckily, too, everybody loves a train. The construction of the railroad soon became a community project that in-

Right, Vista Grande, American-built and the first engine to run on the line in 1967, was one of the two found in Mexico. Left and below, a 1936 German-built Henschel, in regular service. Photographs Fred Busk.

cluded Cripple Creek's newspaper editor, an ex-mayor, and railroaders from the Rio Grande and the Great Western. A thrill ran through the town on June 28, 1967, when the tiny 0-4-0 saddle tanker, named *Vista Grande,* bellowed smoke and steam and puffed down those first 1,000 feet of track.

The railroad was an instant success with both townspeople and tourists. With the revenues, John Birmingham soon expanded the line to four miles, and it now runs through the gold fields to the town of Victor and back.

Cripple Creek & Victor Narrow-Gauge Railroad, P.O. Box 459, Cripple Creek, Colorado 80813; (303) 689-2640. A 45-minute trip backward in time to the lusty pioneer days of railroading during its greatest era. **Schedule:** daily from end-of-May through first weekend in Oct.; trains depart every 45 minutes from 10 A.M. to 5:30 P.M. **Fares:** $4, children $2.50. **Location:** from Denver take I-25 south to Colorado Springs and US-24 west to town of Divide; from there Route 67 goes south to Cripple Creek. **Of special note:** the Imperial Hotel for lodging, its buffet for sustenance, and the Imperial Players for entertainment.

Manitou and Pike's Peak Cog Railway

The highest cog railroad in the world ascends to the 14,100-foot-high summit of Pike's Peak, where the spectacular view has not changed in the least since U.S. Army Lieutenant Zebulon M. Pike first stood there in 1806 and gazed out over the Rocky Mountains, which he had been exploring.

What has changed over the years is the constantly updated equipment of the Manitou and Pike's Peak Cog Railway. Zalmon Simmons, the mattress king, established the railroad in 1890 to haul Colorado tourists to the top of the mountain for the thrill of a lifetime. Regular locomotives could not negotiate the steep inclines, so the railroad had to be specially constructed. The cog locomotive that was decided upon has a gear underneath that engages teeth embedded in a center rail and pulls the locomotive forward without slippage on even the steepest grades. A perfect safety record has been maintained over the past 100 years.

The ride begins at the Base Station depot, which was built in 1890 and is still in use today. From the depot in Manitou Springs, at elevation 6,571 feet, the railroad twists and turns on its eight-mile trip to the summit. The round trip takes a little over three hours, including forty minutes at the summit for sight-seeing, refreshments, and purchasing souvenirs.

In the clear, unpolluted air of Pike's Peak, the word sightseeing takes on a special meaning. It is possible to see Denver 75 miles to the north, New Mexico 100 miles to the south, and, just to the west, Cripple Creek, the great old mining town that has a narrow-gauge railroad of its own.

At first, steam supplied the motive power on the railroad, in the form of tiny, specially designed tank locomotives. Now used only on special occasions, the steam engines did a heroic job until 1955, when streamlined diesel trains took over. These in turn were replaced in 1968 by Swiss-made diesel railcars painted in new, brilliant red livery. More Swiss trains joined the roster in 1976 when articulated double cars that are hinged in the middle were introduced. At the same time, passing sidings were added, allowing more trips each day so the railroad could cope with the increased popularity of the magnificent ride.

Where sightseeing takes on a special meaning

Left, a new Swiss rail car above the tree line on a 95-year-old trip to the summit and right, the interior. Right below, one of the old steam engines, now retired.

Manitou and Pike's Peak Railway Co., P.O. Box 1329, Colorado Springs, Colorado 80901; (303) 685-5401. Climb to the summit on the highest cog railway in the world for an unparalleled view. **Schedule:** varies through the year, but in summer earliest leaves 8 A.M., latest returns 8:30 P.M. All year there is a 9:20 A.M. and 1:20 P.M., returning at 12:30 P.M. and 4:30 P.M. Call in advance to confirm reservations, schedule, and weather. **Fares:** $13.00, children $5.75. **Location:** depot at 515 Ruxton Ave., Manitou Springs. Exit 141 off I-25 west to Manitou Springs on US-24. Exit at signs onto Manitou Ave. to Ruxton. Turn left 1 mile to depot. **Of special note:** a special cable car up Manitou incline, with a grade of 68 per cent and a wonderful view.

A mecca for narrow-gauge railroad enthusiasts

Cumbres & Toltec Scenic Railroad

Left, No. 484 eastbound across Cascade Creek trestle near Osier, Colorado. Below, a double header thunders past Cresco water tank on the state line between Chama and Cumbres. Photographs Ernest Robart.

The nineteenth-century operators of the gold and silver mines buried deep in Colorado's Rocky Mountains desperately needed a railroad to bring in supplies and take out the treasure. In the 1870s an adventurous entrepreneur named General William Jackson Palmer seized the opportunity and built 500 miles of tortuous track that twisted and turned in all directions as it wended its way around, between, under, and over the massive expanse of craggy mountains. Palmer built the tracks of this major American railroad, the Denver and Rio Grande, to a gauge of 3 feet rather than the standard gauge of 4 feet, 8½ inches. The narrower gauge allowed for much sharper curves and reduced the amount of drilling, blasting, and earth-moving necessary to make the roadbed, cutting construction costs in half. The new line was so spectacular that since it was built the term ''narrow gauge'' has been synonymous with mountain railroads, even though there are narrow-gauge railroads in other terrains as well.

Over the years, most of the original railroad from Denver was converted to standard gauge so it could be linked with the other major railroads. Only the section between Alamosa and Durango and the branch lines to Farmington and Silverton are still narrow gauge. This part

*Left, passing a track gang at Cumbres Pass. **Below,** double header climbing the 4 per cent grade one-half mile east of Lobato Bridge. **Below far left,** climbing a grade at Lobo Lodge. Photographs Ernest Robart. **Below left,** photograph Ron Johnson.*

of the country has become a kind of mecca for railroad enthusiasts who want to watch and photograph antique steam trains operating as they did in the last century.

In 1967 the Denver and Rio Grande received permission to abandon its narrow-gauge railway, and avid fans of the Iron Horse organized to save the line over Cumbres Pass. They convinced the states of Colorado and New Mexico to purchase the most scenic segment—the sixty-four miles between Chama, Colorado, and Antonito, New Mexico.

The Cumbres and Toltec Scenic Railroad—named after Cumbres Pass and the Toltec Gorge, the two most scenic spots on the railroad—came into being in 1971. In 1982, managing the railroad was turned over to Kyle Railways, which also operates numerous other tourist railroads, because the two states did not have the expertise to run a scenic railroad.

The railroad has nine steam locomotives, but the workhorses of the line are several 2-8-2 Mikados built in 1925 by the Baldwin Locomotive Works in Philadelphia. When loaded with coal and water, each weighs 143 tons. The railroad is replacing the last of the old converted wooden passenger cars with new, custom-built coaches. One of the most no-

Antonito, Colorado

ticeable old structures at Chama is a wooden coal "tipple," or loading tower, the last one of its kind still operating in the United States. The old brick roundhouse at Chama houses some of the new line's locomotives and its repair facilities.

Because the Cumbres and Toltec Scenic Railroad uses antique equipment and passes through such dramatic scenery, studios often use it to film westerns. Recently, *The Lone Ranger, Bite the Bullet, Shootout, Missouri Breaks,* and *The Good Guys and the Bad Guys* were shot on the railroad.

Cumbres & Toltec Scenic Railroad, P.O. Box 789, Chama, New Mexico 87520; (505) 756-2151; P.O. Box 668, Antonito, Colorado 81120; (303) 376-5483. Another narrow-gauge section of the famous Denver & Rio Grande Western, running through the mountains between 2 states. **Schedule:** trains run daily from mid-June to mid-October—*The Colorado Limited* from Antonito, Col., to Osier, Col., and back via Toltec Gorge and Los Pinos River Valley; *New Mexico Express* from Chama, N.M., to Osier and back via Wolf Creek and Cumbres Pass. Write for exact schedule. **Fares:** $24, children $9. **Location:** Chama is in New Mexico at junction of US-84 and N.M. Route 17; Antonito, is in Colorado just north of the N.M. border on US-285. **Of special note:** the great old Denver & Rio Grande Mikados heading up 4 percent grades.

Left, No. 484 departing Chama, New Mexico, rail yards. **Above,** the old Denver & Rio Grande Western depot and track at Antonito, Colorado, as it once appeared. Track at right curves off to Chama, New Mexico, and track to left once took trains to Santa Fe before 1941. Photographs Ernest Robart. **Right,** pause for a stretch at the Cumbres section house. Photograph Ron Johnson.

Above, a striking view of the Silverton-bound train snaking through the Animas Canyon (photograph D&S RR), and, *far right,* the River of Lost Souls at the bottom of the canyon, with the train running precariously alongside. *Right,* author Terry Berger boards the train at Durango. *Center right,* the departing train headed by one of the famous narrow-gauge Mikados. Photographs Fred Busk.

Durango & Silverton Narrow-Gauge Railroad

Where mountain railroading reaches its zenith

The legendary Durango-to-Silverton narrow-gauge railroad is probably the best scenic tourist train in the world. Here mountain railroading reaches its zenith as the narrow-gauge line follows the Animas Canyon and Gorge. The scenery is magnificent! Accessible only by railroad, horseback, or foot, the route provides spectacular views as the train snakes along the High Line, a narrow shelf blasted out of the red granite 400 feet above the water below.

The Denver & Rio Grande Railroad constructed the forty-five-mile section from Durango to Silverton to haul rich deposits of gold and silver out of the San Juan Mountains. Completed in 1882, it was a money-saver, enabling the mining companies to eliminate the ore-carrying wagons that lumbered over two towering mountain passes. It is estimated that more than $300 million in precious metals rode these rails.

During the late 1960s, when the Denver & Rio Grande Western was permitted to abandon the narrow-gauge tracks from Antonito north to Durango, the forty-five miles of track from Durango to Silverton were cut off from the rest of the system. The company sold the Silverton branch with all its rolling stock, its station, and its roundhouse in 1981.

Charles E. Bradshaw, Jr., who purchased the railroad, is a citrus grower from Orlando, Florida. He has an overflowing love for the railroad and coffers to match. He has lavished extraordinary amounts of time, money, and loving care on the railroad. A stickler for authentic

Overleaf, a closeup of two Mikados double heading a train along a rock cut through the Animas Canyon.

restoration, he has replaced smoke stacks on the locomotives, maintained hand-firing, laid new rails, strengthened bridges, and rebuilt original Denver & Rio Grande cars to near perfection. He is currently building three or four new cars a year from scratch, to 1880s Denver and Rio Grande specifications in state-of-the-art woodworking and metal shops staffed by extraordinary carpenters.

Three locomotives operate out of Durango daily, a phenomenon among tourist railroads. They are all Mikados, with 2-8-2 wheel arrangements but of varying tractive power. In addition, a 105-year-old Jackson & Sharp parlor car, now a common coach, was rebuilt in 1981 as the Alamosa, an elegant parlor car with bar. It offers first-class service. Finally, the railroad is in the process of restoring an old, 1880s Baldwin 2-8-0 Consolidation from the Rio Grande Southern, which Bradshaw bought recently and is the only one left of its kind.

An amazingly complete guidebook that is for sale on the train charts the trip mile by mile, historically and geologically. It is keyed into mileposts along the way and may be obtained in advance from the railroad.

Because thousands of vacationers and railroad enthusiasts ride the train each year, and there are always long lines at the station, it is wise to make reservations far in advance. This train is so popular that people have been known to move to the area, from just about anywhere, to be near it.

Through the mountains to Silverton. Photograph Fred Busk.

Durango & Silverton Narrow-Gauge Railroad, 479 Main Avenue, Durango, Colorado 81301; (303) 247-2733. Two trips through the mountains and canyons of legendary mining country, the railroad being famous as part of the old Denver & Rio Grande Western Railroad. **Schedule:** Durango-Silverton 8-hr. trip daily all year, except Christmas Eve and Day with 3 trains in summer departing 7:30, 8:30, 9:30 A.M. returning in afternoon; Durango-Cascade Canyon trip is 4 hrs. return, departing 4:30 P.M. in summer, 9:55 A.M. in winter. There are such crowds riding these trains it is necessary to reserve and obtain tickets in advance by mail; further details on schedules should be obtained at that time. **Fares:** Silverton return $24.45, children $12.25, parlor car (over 21) $42; Cascade Canyon return $20.70, children $10.35, parlor car (over 21) $34.50. **Location:** Durango is in the Rocky Mountains in the southwest corner of Colorado. **Of special note:** Durango's Strater Hotel, restored to revive nostalgia for the "good old days" of the wild west; Silverton, a refurbished western mining town.